The New Basel Capital Accord and SME Financing

The New Basel Capital Accord and SME Financing

SMEs and the New Rating Culture

Rym Ayadi

November 2005

The Centre for European Policy Studies (CEPS) is an independent policy research institute in Brussels. Its mission is to produce sound policy research leading to constructive solutions to the challenges facing Europe. As a research institute, CEPS takes no position on matters of policy. The views expressed are entirely those of the author.

Acknowledgments: The author would like to thank Els Desmet, Ortwin Volcke and Karel Lannoo for their constructive comments and suggestions along with all those who contributed to the finalisation of this report by responding to the CEPS survey on the Basel II Capital Accord and SME financing. CEPS gratefully acknowledges financial support for this study from CRION, a member of Aon Trade Credit. The report, however, is the responsibility of the author and any conclusions should not be attributed to CRION.

ISBN 92-9079-591-3

Centre for European Policy Studies
Place du Congrès 1, B-1000 Brussels
Tel: (32.2) 229.39.11 Fax: (32.2) 219.41.51
E-mail: info@ceps.be

CONTENTS

List of Tables

List of Figures

List of Boxes

EXECUTIVE SUMMARY AND RECOMMENDATIONS

As the negotiating period for finalising the new Basel Capital Accord (hereafter 'Basel II') drew to a close, there were serious apprehensions among industry members that the likely high capital charge would discourage banks from granting loans to small- and medium-sized enterprises (SMEs), thereby triggering a shortage of finance for this sector. It was thought that this situation would damage the EU economy since SMEs, which are known to be the most important source of growth and employment creation in the EU, already suffer from financing problems. These concerns were partially assuaged when the Basel Committee introduced a more favourable treatment of SME portfolios under pillar 1, based on empirical evidence suggesting that SMEs have a lower default correlation than large enterprises. This finding in turn suggests that the lower the default correlation among SMEs, the fewer the number of firms in this sector that are affected by the same macroeconomic factors and the more the default is related to idiosyncratic or firm-specific risks. Nevertheless, the more risk-sensitive pricing introduced by the internal ratings-based approaches under pillar 1 of Basel II will certainly entail variation in capital adequacy, depending upon the individual quality of the SME. Indeed, a poor-quality (low-rated) SME will force the bank to hold more regulatory capital compared to a high-quality (highly rated) SME. This situation does not curtail loan financing for SMEs, but it does make its availability conditional on the enterprise's financial strength and ability to provide relevant quantitative and qualitative information.

This study discusses the main characteristics of the SME sector in Europe and provides an informative analysis about what Basel II means for SMEs and its impact on their credit financing conditions. It also presents a detailed analysis of how banks formulate an internal rating system and illustrates how this system works in practice. Finally, it concludes with the key measures that should be taken by banks, SMEs and public policy-makers to improve SME financing in the new rating culture. The conclusions of the study are summarised below.

1. *The evolution of SME financing by banks*

Despite the slowdown of the overall growth rate in bank lending to SMEs in the past few years - reflecting the weak economic cycle, reduced demand and more selective lending - banks in Europe seem to see real growth opportunities in the SME lending sector. In parallel, although SMEs have access to a variety of financing sources, including leasing, factoring and trade credit, they rely heavily on bank financing. Nevertheless, several constraints continue to hinder SME financing in line with firms' natural growth cycle. According to banks, the lack of equity, the high credit risk, the paucity of collateral and poor information about the firms constitute the main obstacles to granting finance to SMEs. Other constraints that play a role in the assessment of loan applications, such as poor entrepreneurial capacity, business performance and uncertain development prospects, are felt to be equally important.

Today, bank financing requires a large amount of financial and strategic information that ought to be provided by SMEs to reduce the information deficit between them and their lenders. Faced with implementing the requirements of Basel II worldwide and the new Capital Requirements Directive (CRD) in the EU, banks are expected to require even more and better quality information. The new regulatory rules have introduced more stringent requirements to counter the growing concern of risks at the EU and global levels. This step does not imply credit rationing. Instead, it requires banks to view their business in a more sophisticated and risk-sensitive manner. As a consequence, SMEs need to understand these regulatory changes as they will impact their financing conditions to a certain degree - not necessarily by reducing their credit facilities but by rendering the whole process more risk-sensitive and contingent upon the individual quality of the borrowers.

2. *The future shape of decision-making for bank credit*

Banks derive a credit rating and thus the probability of default associated with the borrower through four stages:

i) the gathering of historical quantitative and qualitative information;
ii) an analysis of the individual factors;
iii) the specification and estimation of the model; and
iv) the determination of the rating and the associated probability of default.

In the first stage, accurate and relevant quantitative and qualitative data are collected. The quantitative data (mainly extracted from financial statements) include: performance, leverage, debt coverage, liquidity, growth, productivity, size and other macroeconomic and political factors as well as a detailed and precise business plan. The qualitative data include: the profile of the enterprise, the development prospects of the industry, the reputation/experience/ability of the entrepreneur and his/her past credit history, the ownership and governance structure, the management quality of accounts receivable and the availability of collateral and guarantees, etc.

These data are traditionally required when SMEs ask for loans under the current Basel regulation (the 1988 Accord). With the implementation of Basel II and the transposition of the CRD into national laws from the end of 2006, banks will ask for *even more information*. This information must be clear, focused, complete, more structured and timely. The decision to grant credit will be highly conditional on the individual quality of the borrower.

Formally, the new banking regulation will have more impact on the second, third and fourth stages of deriving a rating. Indeed, the information submitted will be interpreted using statistical models that extract more decision-relevant information for rating and probability of default. This enhances the bank's ability to identify potential future defaults. Cross-subsidisation between high-quality and poor-quality borrowers will no longer be allowed. In addition, it is expected that the current trend towards collateralised lending as a means to mitigate credit risk and to allow the calculation of recovery rates is likely to rise.

3. *Practical effects of Basel II and the CRD on SME financing*

The new banking capital rules will directly affect three components of the cost of credit to SMEs, as follows:

- The *administrative/operational costs* resulting from processes to initiate and manage loan portfolios may increase, owing to the use of more sophisticated risk-management tools that require a greater investment in human resources and infrastructure (to undertake data collection, database maintenance and adequate modelling, for example).

- The rules will also have an impact on the *cost of risk*, composed of the cost of capital, which is the opportunity cost resulting from the fact that banks need regulatory and risk capital to cover loan exposures.
- Finally, there will be an effect on the *risk premium*, which is linked to the probability of default of the borrower, the exposure at default and the loss-given default.

The impact of the new banking regulatory rules on the cost of risk and the risk premium is not straightforward since it will largely depend on the risk characteristics of the borrowers.

The more risk-sensitive pricing introduced by the new rules through the internal ratings-based approaches will entail a certain variation in capital adequacy, which is ultimately related to the individual quality of the borrowers. A poor-quality borrower will force its lender to hold more regulatory capital compared with a better-quality borrower, but this does not reduce loan financing.

4. *The role of banks and the key success factors for a better financing relationship between banks and SMEs*

Enhanced transparency, structured dialogue, openness and communication are the cornerstones of an effective cooperation between banks and SMEs. These principles will ensure a successful financing relationship.

Banks should not hesitate to play their role and increase transparency with their customers by showing them how ratings impact their credit terms. Communication should not be limited to the reasons for not granting bank loans or withdrawing existing lines of credit. Rather, it should be built upon mutual trust between banks and SMEs. Bank procedures including individual rating, risk assessment and factors for downgrading or upgrading credit risk *need to be more transparent* to SMEs.

Disclosing the key elements of the risk assessment process is necessary to allow loan applicants to understand bank decisions (rejection, acceptance, improved or worsening financing conditions, etc.). In the meantime, explaining the overall, detailed risk-assessment process should not create an extra burden for the bank since the extra cost of mobilising additional human resources could be passed on to the SMEs.

It is notable, however, that as the application of different internal rating methodologies (the foundation versus the advanced internal ratings approaches) will imply different ratings for the same quality of borrower, the disclosure of individual ratings to loan applicants may result in a competitive disadvantage for those banks that should normally be rewarded for their use of the most sophisticated internal models to rate credit risk and detect potentially bad borrowers.

Although the key elements disclosed should be clearly defined, it is not necessary at this stage to explicitly regulate the disclosure of ratings to loan applicants. A non-legislative code of conduct between banks and SMEs should suffice to establish a framework that sets out the principles for rating-process disclosure for banking and SME associations.

5. *The role of SMEs and the practical actions they can take to improve their financing conditions*

The steps that SMEs need to take are obviously expected to be even greater than banks. SMEs need to be aware of the changing banking environment. Indeed, this awareness will increase their ability to identify better financing options.

When applying for a loan from an internal ratings-based bank, an enterprise needs to signal its creditworthiness by providing clear, focused, complete, well-structured and timely quantitative and qualitative information. This information is the key to running the internal ratings system properly. Companies that are well-managed, adequately leveraged (equity ratio) and that provide such information will be in a position to obtain a good rating and consequently better credit conditions.

In practice, SMEs must:

- provide timely, relevant and precise financial data and demonstrate financial performance needed by lenders to assign yearly ratings. Delayed submission of financial and performance data is seen to be a warning signal by many banks' internal rating systems. It usually leads to a downgrading of creditworthiness and therefore price increases in loan offers or the refusal of new loans;
- improve the factors that are considered to be important in the ratings process, such as:
    - cash-flow stabilisation and generation;
    - company accounting, control and management methods;

  - the equity base, by giving preference to retained earnings over distributed profits;
  - consolidation of the business development strategy;
  - strategic thinking among managers in terms of business prospects and market/sector/activity analyses;
  - external communications with stakeholders;
  - provision of adequate guarantees and collaterals;
  - attention given to some aspects of the business that may have been neglected so far;
  - establishment of recovery procedures in case of distress scenarios;
- take more active measures to increase equity finance; and
- consider alternative financing sources to banks, such as leasing, factoring or other means that could offer a good response to SMEs.

6. The role of public policy-makers to intervene when necessary

It is important to continue improving the relationship between banks and SMEs in terms of a better rating culture by developing a non-legislative framework that sets out the principles to define the minimum criteria for ratings disclosure. Moreover, since a stronger equity base is an indicator of better creditworthiness, it is important to ensure greater access to equity finance and to offer more tax incentives to use retained earnings to increase the equity base. Finally, the legislative efforts to combat habitual late payments and thus stabilise cash flows should continue and be reinforced.

INTRODUCTION

It is widely accepted that the SME sector plays a central role in promoting employment, growth and innovation in Europe. Therefore, it is very important to ensure that financing conditions for SMEs are not overly tight because of more stringent capital rules, particularly when they already have difficulties in accessing finance in capital markets given their limited size and reputation.

SMEs in a number of EU countries have expressed concerns about the likely impact that the European version of the new Basel Capital Accord (Basel II) and the Capital Requirements Directive (CRD) could have on their access to credit and the related costs that this may entail. In this context it is useful to start with a brief history of the treatment of SME financing under Basel II.

In July 2002, the Basel Committee agreed to grant loans to SMEs under a special and more favourable treatment framework. According to the current Basel II and CRD proposals, SME funding by the banks using either the standardised or internal ratings-based (IRB) approach will in general be given a lower capital requirement than loans to larger firms. The capital savings, which may be as high as 20%, result from the application of a reduction mechanism (discount factor) that corrects the asset risk weights on the basis of the borrower's size.[1] By allowing this special regime, the Basel Committee finally put an end to the long and heated debate that had flared up, particularly across Europe, after the release of the second consultation paper in January 2001.

[1] The firm-size adjustment factor is an algorithm that modifies the asset correlation in reverse proportion to the SME's size.

In theory, the SMEs' concerns should have disappeared after they were accorded this preferential regulatory capital treatment. In practice, however, the new Capital Accord has introduced a very risk-selective approach: indeed, the more risk a borrower entails, the higher the capital charge will be. In other words, an SME that has a good business plan but inadequate equity and volatile cash-flows will accrue a higher cost of credit.

These concerns still have some foundation, as little is known about the immediate implications of new regulations when they are first introduced. These concerns may be alleviated, however, by becoming informed about the new regulation, its likely implications and the way in which banks will use internal rating systems to assess SME creditworthiness.

This study discusses the main characteristics of the SME sector in Europe and provides an analysis of what Basel II means for SMEs and its impact on their credit financing conditions. It also presents a detailed look at how banks formulate an internal rating system and illustrates how this system works in practice. Finally, it concludes with the key measures that should be taken by banks, SMEs and public policy-makers to improve SME financing in the new rating culture. Some recommendations are also given in the course of the analysis, not only for SMEs to accommodate the new rating culture but also addressed to the competent authorities to ensure that the new rules do not jeopardise the SME sector and in turn the European economy.

1. An overview of the SME sector in Europe

SMEs play a key role in the European economy: they are an essential source of jobs and they foster innovation and growth. Therefore, it is crucial to ensure that they have access to credit. Several financing sources are available to them, but banking credit has traditionally been and will continue to be the chief source of their funding. Nevertheless, SMEs continue to suffer from a position of weakness when applying for a loan.

1.1 A European definition of an SME

In 1990, the European Commission began to develop an EU definition of SME. The demand for a harmonised definition was initiated by the Industry Council, to overcome the limitations of varying SME definitions that had been used in the past. The Commission's definition was released in May 2003 and took effect in January 2005. It is based on four criteria as outlined below (see also Table 1).

1) Staff headcounts or number of employees, which are established in annual work units (AWU). Anyone who worked full-time within the enterprise, or on its behalf, during the entire reference year counts as one unit. Part-time staff, seasonal workers and those who did not work the full year are treated as part-time staff, i.e. as fractions of one unit. The staff headcounts cover:
   - employees;
   - other persons working for the enterprise who are subordinate to it and considered to be employees under national law;
   - owner-managers;
   - partners who are engaged in a regular activity in the enterprise and who benefit from financial advantages arising from it.
2) Annual turnover, which is determined by calculating the income that the enterprise earned during the year in question from its sales and services after any rebates have been paid out. Turnover should not include value added taxes (VAT) or other indirect taxes.
3) Balance sheet total, along with reference to the value of the company's assets.
4) Independence, which is another criterion to complement the definition of an independent (autonomous) or partner or linked micro, small- or medium-sized enterprise. This is defined in terms of capital and voting rights. An enterprise is considered to be independent when the influence of a single shareholder is limited. It is also considered independent if it has no participation in other enterprises and no enterprise has participation in it, or if the enterprise has a holding of less than 25% of the capital or voting rights in one or more other enterprises and/or outsiders do not have a stake of more than 25% of the capital or voting rights in it. This criterion permits calculations in the cases of independent, partner or linked enterprises and will ultimately determine whether or not the enterprise in question meets the various thresholds established in the SME definition.[2]

[2] For more details, see European Commission (2005a).

Table 1. EU definition of an SME

Category	Staff headcounts (annual work units – AWU)	Annual turnover	Annual balance sheet total	Independence
Micro	<10	€2 million	€2 million	Given by <25% of
Small	<50	€10 million	€10 million	capital shares held
Medium-sized	<250	€ 50 million	€43 million	by a third party

Source: European Commission (2003c).

An enterprise should compare its data with the thresholds introduced in the four criteria to enable it to identify itself among one of the three sub-categories in the SME sector: micro, small or medium-sized.[3] As Table 1 shows, micro, small and medium-sized enterprises consist of those that employ fewer than 250 persons and have either an annual turnover not exceeding €50 million **or** an annual balance-sheet total not exceeding €43 million.

Under the established categories, medium-sized enterprises are defined as those that employ more than 50 but fewer than 250 persons, and whose annual turnover is more than €10 million but less than or equal to €50 million **or** whose annual balance-sheet total is more than €10 million but does not exceed €43 million. Small enterprises are defined as those that employ fewer than 50 persons and whose annual turnover or annual balance-sheet total does not exceed €10 million. Micro-enterprises are defined as those that employ fewer than 10 persons and whose annual turnover or annual balance-sheet total does not exceed €2 million.

It is important to note that while it is compulsory to respect the staff headcount thresholds, an SME may choose to meet either the turnover or balance-sheet ceiling. It does not need to satisfy both and may exceed one of them without losing its status.

---

[3] If the enterprise exceeds the headcounts or financial thresholds during the course of the reference year, its status will not be affected. The enterprise will retain the SME status with which it began that year. It will lose the status, however, if it goes above the thresholds over two consecutive accounting periods. Conversely, an enterprise could gain SME status if it was previously a large enterprise but falls below the thresholds for two consecutive accounting periods.

1.2 The importance of the SME sector in Europe

SMEs play a central role in employment in Europe. According to the Observatory of European SMEs[4] (European Commission, 2002 and 2003), SMEs account for 99% of all companies and provide jobs for more than 90 million persons in the EU-19,[5] accounting for about two-thirds of total employment (Table 2). Among SMEs, the major share of jobs is in micro-enterprises, which employ fewer than 10 employees. This trend has continued since 2000 (see Table 3).

Nevertheless, the size of companies measured in terms of the average number of employees differs considerably among countries. Table 3 provides an indication of the dominant size class of firms by country in the EU in 2003. The average company size seems to be very small, particularly in southern Mediterranean countries such as Greece and Italy. This reflects the large percentage of small family-owned firms in these countries. By contrast, Austria, Ireland, Luxembourg and the Netherlands have the largest average number of employees per firm.

Table 2. The role of SMEs in the EU-19 (2003)

	SMEs	LSEs*	Total
Number of enterprises (x 1,000)	19,270	40	19,310
Employment (x 1,000)	97,420	42,300	139,710
Persons employed by enterprise (on average)	5	1,052	
Turnover per enterprise (€ million)	0.9	319	
Value added per employee (per €1,000)	55	120	
Share of labour costs in value added (%)	56	47	

* Large-scale enterprises.

Sources: Estimated by EIM Business and Policy Research, based on Eurostat's SME database; also based on *European Economy*, Supplement A, May 2003 and *Economic Outlook*, No. 71, OECD, June 2003.

[4] The European Commission's Observatory of European SMEs regularly publishes information on SMEs across the EU-15, as well as Iceland, Liechtenstein, Norway and Switzerland.

[5] The EU-19 comprises the EU-15 plus Iceland, Liechtenstein, Norway and Switzerland.

Table 3. Size of enterprises in the EU-19 by country (2003)

	Enterprises (1000s)	Average enterprise size (employed persons per enterprise)	Size class dominance*
Austria	270	11	Micro
Belgium	440	7	Micro
Denmark	210	10	SME
Finland	220	7	LSE
France	2,500	8	Micro
Germany	3,020	10	LSE
Greece	770	2	Micro
Ireland	100	10	SME
Italy	4,490	4	Micro
Luxembourg	20	9	SME
Netherlands	570	12	LSE
Portugal	690	5	SME
Spain	2,680	6	Micro
Sweden	490	7	Micro
UK	2,230	11	LSE
EU-15	**18,700**	**7**	**Micro**
Iceland	30	4	LSE
Norway	240	7	SME
Liechtenstein	4	6	Micro
Switzerland	340	8	SME
Non-EU	610	7	SME
Total EU-19	19,310	7	Micro

* A country or sector of industry is said to be micro, small, medium-sized or LSE-dominated if either micro, small and medium-sized (taken together) or large-scale enterprises have the largest share in total employment (in number).

When comparing productivity and development of the workforce as well as the profitability of SMEs with large-scale enterprises (LSEs) over the period 1988-2001, SMEs showed satisfactory growth in productivity, contributed to an overall increase in employment and experienced a higher increase in average profitability than LSEs[6] (Table 4). These data provide substantial evidence of the growth potential offered by SMEs to the European economy.

[6] The data for 1988-2003 confirm the same trend (Observatory of European SMEs, 2003-07).

Yet major constraints continue to hinder their business performance and growth. According to the ENSR[7] surveys conducted for the European Observatory of SMEs in 2002[8] among 7,669 SMEs in 19 European countries, the lack of skilled labour and poor access to finance are major problems. The same survey in 2003 showed that the paucity of customer purchasing power has also put the brake on SME business growth alongside the constraints listed in 2002. While the low level of customer purchasing power is a direct result of the unfavourable economic climate, the core issues of access to skilled labour and finance are persistent factors.

Table 4. SMEs' real value-added employment and profitability by country, EU-19 in 1988-2001 (average annual change in %)

	Real value added		**Employment**		**Profitability**	
	SMEs	**LSEs**	**SMEs**	**LSEs**	**SMEs**	**LSEs**
Austria	2.2	1.9	0	0.2	0.1	-0.1
Belgium	1.9	2.2	0.2	0	0.1	0.4
Denmark	2.6	2.8	0.1	0.2	0.6	0.7
Finland	-0.1	0.1	-1.7	-1.6	-1.3	-1.2
France	1.3	2.4	0.3	0.7	-0.1	0.2
Germany	2.5	3.2	0.3	-0.3	0.3	0.6
Greece	3.3	2.3	2.1	1	-0.6	-3
Ireland	7.7	9.5	2.8	3.1	2.1	0.9
Italy	1.3	1.3	-0.3	-0.4	1.1	1.5
Luxembourg	5.4	4.8	2.6	1.1	0	0.4
Netherlands	2.1	2.5	1.1	0.9	0	0.3
Portugal	3	3.3	0.2	0.4	2.6	0.7
Spain	2.7	2.9	1.2	1.3	0.4	0.4
Sweden	1.6	0.8	-1.2	-1.4	0.1	-0.9
UK	2.4	2.3	-0.1	-0.9	0.2	0.2
EU-15	2	2.5	0.3	-0.1	0.5	0.3
Iceland	1.6	0	1.3	0.5	-0.6	2.7
Norway	3.2	3.9	1.5	1.5	0.2	1.1
Switzerland	1.6	1.7	0.4	0.1	0.5	2.1
Non-EU	2.2	2.5	0.7	0.4	0.3	2
Total	2.1	2.6	0.3	-0.1	0.5	0.3

Sources: Estimated by EIM Business and Policy Research, based on Eurostat's SME database; also based on *European Economy*, Supplement A, June 2001 and *Economic Outlook*, No. 65, OECD, June 2001.

---

[7] ENSR refers to the European Network for SME Research.

[8] See European Commission (2002).

Table 5. Main activities of SMEs by country in 2002 (in %)*

	AT	BE	DK	DE	EL	ES	FR	FI	IE	IT	LU	NL	PT	SE	UK	EU-19
Manufacturing	12	9	14	9	4	10	9	13	9	15	4	8	14	11	10	11
Construction	8	13	14	10	14	11	13	13	18	12	9	9	16	10	22	13
Wholesale trade	8	12	12	7	11	8	6	9	6	9	13	10	9	11	4	7
Retail trade	9	23	16	15	49	23	17	14	20	19	13	16	30	9	9	18
Hotels & catering	16	11	2	5	6	8	11	1	1	6	13	6	10	1	2	6
Repair	10	1	6	3	1	1	2	2	1	2	2	3	3	8	3	3
Transport & communications	5	4	6	4	5	9	4	12	6	5	5	6	3	6	6	6
Financial services	1	3	4	4	2	1	3	4	1	1	4	3		5	4	2
Business services	16	16	17	22	5	18	21	16	19	20	26	22	10	31	21	19
Other services industries	16	8	10	22	4	11	14	16	19	12	11	18	5	8	19	15
Total	100	100	100	100	100	100	100	100	100	100	100	100	100	100	100	100

* The NACE Rev. 1 nomenclature has been used for business sectors.

Source: ENSR Enterprise Survey in 2002.

In Europe, SMEs operate in a variety of sectors ranging from manufacturing, construction, retail trade and business services (accounting for the largest shares) to financial services (accounting for the smallest share). At country level, business services are particularly relevant in Sweden (more than 30% of SMEs) as well as in the Netherlands, Luxembourg and Germany (more than 20%). Retail trade is important for SMEs in Greece (about 50%), Portugal (30%) Belgium and Spain (more than 20%) (see Table 5).

1.3 Sources of SME financing

Financing an SME generally depends on its sector of activity and its growth cycle.[9] In order to grow, a firm needs to be able to rely on equity and debt. Thus SMEs have a financial growth cycle in which financial needs and options change as the business grows and becomes more transparent.

Figure 1 shows this cycle in a stylised fashion, whereby firms lie on a size/age/information continuum. It seeks to give a general idea of which sources of finance become important at different stages in the financial growth cycle and the points in the cycle at which different types of funding are shown to begin and end.

At the beginning of the growth cycle, the financing of smaller and younger firms is heavily dependent on initial **insider finance** (equity) and external investors through, for example, **angel financing**.[10] (At this stage, these firms are an unknown quantity because they do not yet have a track record and therefore have much difficulty in accessing intermediated external finance.) Insider finance or equity is defined as funds provided by the start-up team, family or friends prior to and at the time of the firm's inception. Angel financing is an informal, non-intermediated market for direct finance where 'angels', who are by definition high net worth individuals, invest directly in small companies through an equity contract, typically common stock. Angels sometimes work as a small investment group in which they coordinate their investment activities.[11] Sometimes this is done in conjunction with lawyers and accountants, who bring deal flair to the group and help structure the contracts.

---

[9] See Berger & Udell (1998).

[10] See Sahlman (1990) and Wetzel (1994).

[11] See Prowse (1998).

Figure 1. Firm continuum and sources of finance

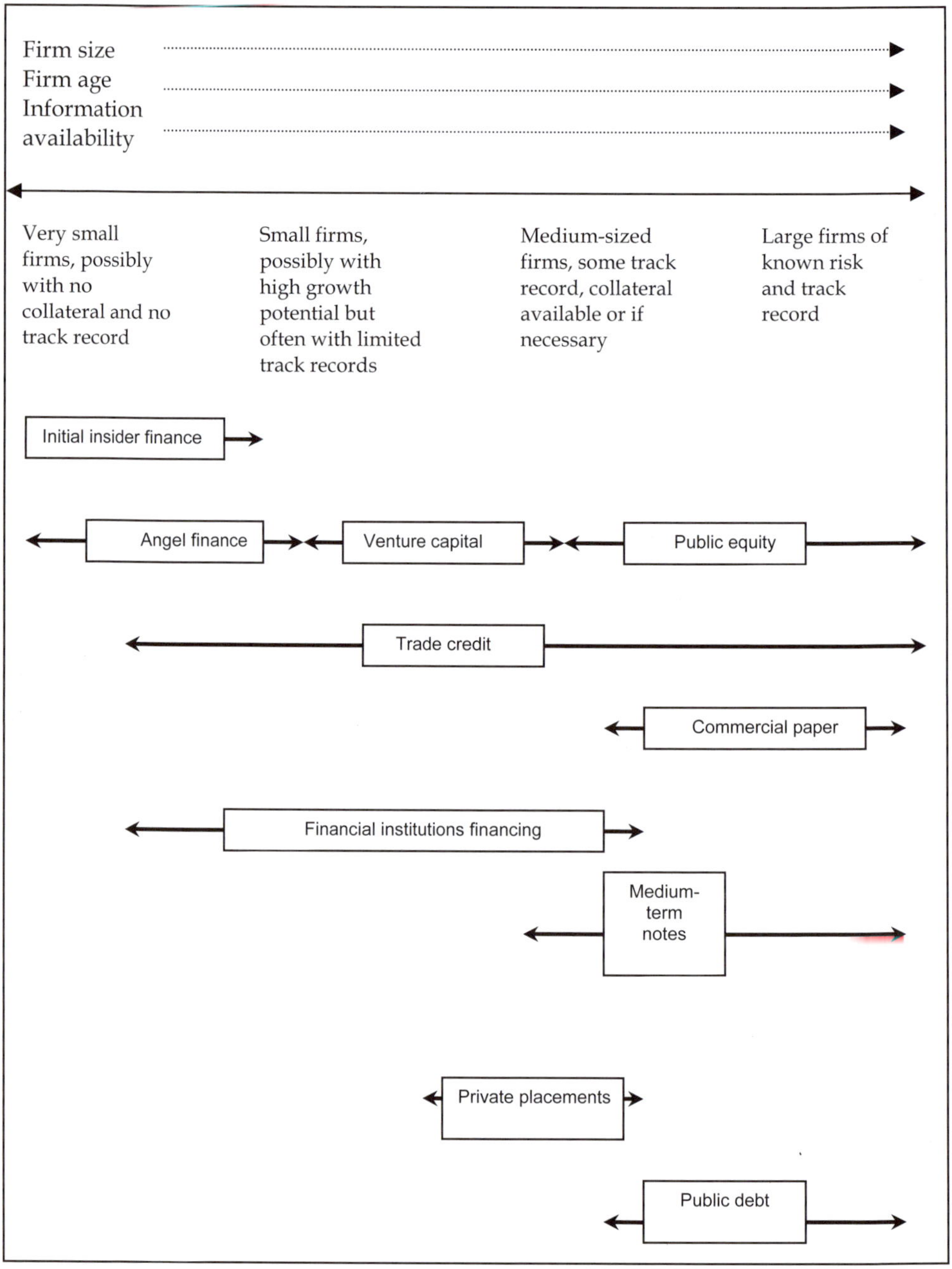

Source: Berger & Udell (1998).

As firms grow, they gain access to intermediated finance on the equity side through **venture capital,** for example, and on the debt side through financial institutions and supplier credit. Venture capital (and trade credit) could typically come after the product or service has been successfully tested by the market and may be used to finance full-scale marketing and production. Eventually, if the firms survive and grow, they may access public equity and debt markets.

Trade (or supplier) credit is the credit the supplier gives to his client in a business-to-business relationship. Instead of paying for the goods and services rapidly in cash, the firm makes delayed payments to its suppliers, which creates the equivalent of a loan from the suppliers to the firm. The use of supplier credit depends on the length of payment period, the availability of the supplier's own funds and also access to bank loans.

Suppliers are generally reluctant to grant trade credit to start-ups because of the lack of information about the firm and the higher probability of default. When companies grow and show stable cash-flows, trade credit becomes a viable and frequently used source of financing.

As firms continue to grow and achieve a level of production whereby their balance sheets reflect substantial, tangible business assets that could be pledged as collaterals and guarantees, they can tap other sources to obtain debt financing. Commercial, cooperative and savings banks, specialised finance companies and other financial institutions together provide most of the external debt finance.

Financial institutions provide two types of credit to SMEs: i) credit cards and credit lines,[12] and ii) mortgage loans,[13] equipment loans, motor vehicle loans, capital leases[14] and other types of loans. The former are typically used to finance working capital needs and are often collateralised by assets unrelated to the use of the credit line. Indeed, they could be guaranteed by one or more insider owners, which gives the financial

---

[12] The credit lines represent a loan commitment by the financial institution to provide future credit (these commitments may include short-term credit including overdrafts and long-term credit).

[13] Mortgages include both commercial and residential mortgages if the funds were used for business purposes. They may be secured by either commercial property or the personal property of the owner.

[14] For most equipment loans, motor vehicle loans and capital leases, the proceeds of the loan or lease are used to purchase the assets pledged as collateral.

institution the possibility of recourse to the personal wealth of the owners in the event the loan is not repaid. In many cases, the personal assets of the owners are explicitly pledged as collateral to back the loans (see Box 1). The latter are typically used to finance specific assets and are collateralised by the assets being financed (commonly known as 'asset-based financing') such as accounts receivable, inventory and equipment.

Box 1. Differences between collaterals and guarantees

Collaterals and guarantees are powerful tools that allow the financial institutions to offer credit on favourable terms (since the collateral itself reduces the risk of the loan) and also to proceed to recovery in the event that the borrower is defaulting on his or her payments. Indeed, providing collateral or a guarantee is not only a pledge against default for the financial institution, but it is also a tool to reduce the informational opacity of small businesses. The lack of information might result in credit rationing or the extension of credit only on relatively unfavourable terms.

There are two types of collateral: the collateral that involves pledged assets owned by the firms (these may include accounts receivable and/or inventory, referred to as 'asset-based lending') and the collateral that involve pledging assets owned outside the firm, typically assets belonging to the firm's owners. The monitoring of receivables and inventory may also produce valuable information about a firm's future performance as well as information about the value of the collateral, which can be used as part of an overall relationship that may lead to more favourable credit terms in the future.

Guarantees give the lender general recourse against the assets of the principle owner or other party issuing the guarantee. A guarantee is similar to a pledge of outside personal collateral, but it differs in two important ways. First, it is a broader claim than the pledge of personal collateral since the liability of the guarantor is not limited to any specific asset. Second, a guarantee is a weaker claim than a pledge of collateral, against any given set of assets since a guarantee does not involve specific terms that prevent these assets from being sold or consumed.

Specialised finance companies also play a key role in providing debt financing to SMEs.

Leasing involves a lease contract, i.e. an agreement between the owner of the asset, 'the lessor', and the user of the asset, the 'lessee', which conveys to the user the right to use the asset in return for a number of specified payments over the agreed period of time. Leasing is simply a way of acquiring an asset without paying cash, taking out a loan or using other forms of financing. For many SMEs, leasing is attractive because it frees up cash that would otherwise be tied up in fixed assets and would not be available to finance working capital. Moreover, leasing companies usually do not require collateral. Hence, in an environment where access to capital may be difficult owing to a lack of financial visibility and collateral, leasing may provide a useful complement or substitute to traditional bank financing.

Factoring involves the purchase (at a discount) of the accounts receivable[15] of a firm by a third party (known as a 'factor'). In the case of factoring, the underlying asset is sold to the factor, which means that in the event the borrower becomes insolvent, the underlying asset (the factored accounts receivable) is not part of the bankrupted estate. Obviously, in a factoring relationship, the credit is primarily based on the quality of the underlying accounts, not the quality of the borrower.

Financial institutions and other finance intermediaries often put considerable weight on the financial conditions and reputations of the insider-owners and also on the relationship they have with them when making any investment decision. Generally, the creditworthiness of the enterprise or the entrepreneur is easily evaluated using modern credit-coring techniques when a long credit history, pledgeable assets and personal data are available.

1.4 Use and structure of SME financing in Europe

A higher equity share within an SME could reduce the risk of an investment and provide a firm with wider access to external finance. According to the European Commission,[16] among the different **external financing sources,** those most frequently used are overdrafts, bank loans, leasing and factoring. Other sources include external investors and subventions. Nevertheless, the majority of European SMEs depend strongly on **bank financing** (through bank loans and overdrafts).

The **availability of equity** to SMEs varies among European countries and among the different firm sizes (Table 6). In some countries such as Germany, Italy and Austria, SMEs rely much less on their own capital,

---

[15] That is, the sale payments due from customers.

[16] European Commission (2001).

while in France, Belgium, Spain and Portugal, the share of equity in the total balance sheet ranges between 39% and 42%. These differences can be attributed to differences in taxation, financial systems and legal frameworks (including the minimum equity requirements for some companies such as start-ups). History and culture play an important role, especially in the case of family ownership and reputation in some specific activities.

Table 6. Share of equity in the total balance sheet by enterprise size (%)

Size by turnover (millions)	Austria	Belgium	France	Germany	Italy	Portugal	Spain
Less than €7m	13	40	34	14	26	31	42
Between €7m and €40m	27	38	35	22	25	40	43
€40m and more	31	39	35	31	28	51	37
All sizes	28	39	35	30	27	42	38

Source: European Commission (2001).

In general, **overdrafts** offer short-term lending that can be used at very short notice (or without any notice period at all). Although they are more expensive than bank loans, they are often preferred by enterprises because of their higher flexibility.[17] Banks typically charge 8-20% for overdrafts when there is an explicit agreement on the threshold. This rate could jump even higher when exceeding the agreed amount.

Bank loans have longer maturity and their charges depend on the interest rates. The environment of low interest rates and inflation experienced over the past few years in the economic and monetary union (EMU) have brought down the rates for bank loans. This means that SMEs can obtain medium- and long-term bank loans at rates that vary between 5-7% (which is 3-4% above the interbank rates).[18]

In terms of banking relationships, in several member states such as Austria and Germany, enterprises have traditionally relied on a close relationship with one local bank (the Hausbank), which covers relatively small credit amounts (<€100,000) and is willing to lend even when business

[17] European Commission (2001).

[18] In May 2005 the one-year interbank rates in the euro area (the Euribor-Euro Interbank Offered Rate) were at their lowest level (almost 2%) since the beginning of the 1990s.

conditions are difficult. As shown by the ENSR survey[19] (2002) (see Table 7), 52% of the micro-enterprises rely on one bank, but one-third of the medium-sized enterprises also have a relationship with only one bank. At a country level, Denmark (with approximately 90%) and Norway (with 80%) show the highest percentages of SMEs having credit lines with only one bank. By contrast, in several southern European countries, SMEs tend to have credit lines with several banks. In Spain for example, only about one-third of the SMEs have credit lines with one bank, which is similar to Greece (37%) and Italy (38%).

Table 7. Percentage of SMEs with credit lines, by number of banks and size class in the EU-19

Number of banks	< 10 employees	10-49 employees	50-249 employees
Only one bank	52	39	33
Two to three banks	38	42	31
Four or more banks	6	11	22
No answer	4	7	14
Total*	100	100	100

*The sum of each column is not always 100%, due to the rounding.

Source: ENSR Enterprise Survey (2002).

As for the amount of credit, almost 60% of the SMEs responding to this question in the ENSR survey have bank liabilities of up to €100,000, another 16% have bank liabilities between €100,000 and €500,000, about 3% have bank liabilities between €500,000 and €1 million, and only 1% have more than that. Finally, with regard to the maturity period of their loans, most of the SMEs' largest bank loans have a maturity period of over three years. As Table 8 shows, the focus on short-term financing is most pronounced in the wholesale sector, whereas loans of five years and more are frequently used in the personal services sector.

With respect to alternative financing sources to bank loans, the use of **leasing** seems to be increasing in Europe. It is most often used to acquire goods with a substantial second-hand value (such as cars, real estate, machinery, etc.). The main disadvantage of leasing is that the 'effective' interest rate is usually higher compared with bank loans. Still, leasing is an interesting source of funding especially for SMEs and enterprises that have low revenues but high growth opportunities. In the EU, leasing rose in 2001

[19] European Commission (2003).

by about 8.5% compared with 2000 – in real terms, this equates to €193 billion.[20] In many countries, leasing seems to be used particularly by fast-growing SMEs (especially those in Belgium, Finland, Ireland and Spain).

Table 8. Maturity period for the largest SME bank loans and sector in the EU-19 (%)

	Manu.	Const.	Whole-sale	Retail	Trans-port & comm.	Bus. Service	Pers. Service	Total
< than 6 months	7	7	18	9	5	9	6	8
6 months-1 year	9	7	7	8	8	5	5	7
1-3 years	14	22	14	14	18	17	18	17
3-5 years	26	26	18	23	26	18	16	21
5 years or longer	21	24	22	26	29	28	43	27
No answer	24	15	21	21	14	22	22	20
Total	100	100	100	100	100	100	100	100

Source: ENSR Enterprise Survey (2002).

According to the Observatory of European SMEs (European Commission, 2003), incorporating findings from the Exco Grant & Thornton Survey of European SMEs (2001),[21] about 11% of SMEs in Europe use **factoring**, but considerable differences can still be observed across countries. Whereas it is estimated that 32% of SMEs in France use factoring, it is hardly ever used in Sweden (only 3%).[22] Factoring is considered to be more suitable for small enterprises and on average 50% of the total number of European factoring companies' clients have an annual turnover of less than €2 million, with 91% having less than €15 million.[23] Despite the fact that it has been used for nearly 40 years, the average penetration rate of factoring is relatively low (only 11%). The low penetration rate of factoring can be readily confirmed when looking at the World Bank's *World Factoring Yearbook – 2003*.[24] When measuring the relative importance of factoring to GDP, the factoring rate did not reach 5.4% in Europe[25] in 2002.

---

[20] See Leaseurope (2002).

[21] The survey was based on 4,400 replies from a sample of 42,400 enterprises.

[22] See the *European Business Survey* by Grant Thornton (2001).

[23] Greater London Enterprise Ltd., *Analysis of Use of Factoring*, Brussels (2003).

[24] See World Bank (2004).

[25] This includes the EU-25 plus Iceland, Norway, Russia, Switzerland and Turkey.

Finally, the use of **trade credit** has been growing among European SMEs (see Table 9). In a survey[26] conducted by Intrum Justitia (2005), trade credit was ranked as the primary financing source above bank and other debt financing. Indeed, for a considerable number of SMEs, trade credit is a more important source of working capital than bank loans.

Table 9. Amounts owed to trade creditors due and payable within one year, 2000 (percentage of total capital)

	Manufacturing[b]		**Retail trade[c]**		**Transportation/Communication[d]**	
Firm size	**Small**	**Medium**	**Small**	**Medium**	**Small**	**Medium**
Austria	12.01[a]	8.53	21.17[a]	15.36	16.12[a]	9.49
Belgium	17.18	20.98	21.11	28.84	17.55	22.97
France	25.55	25.88	28.70	32.5	24.78	19.23
Finland	7.36	3.92	20.47	13.4	11.12	5.72
Germany	13.23	10.80	24.21	19.01	na	na
Italy	23.94	26.46	31.82	39.99	13.89	21.76
Netherlands	na	8.37	na	7.75	na	7.3
Portugal	16.05	15.56	27.73	26.78	10.61	3.5
Spain	21.04	19.33	27.35	26.33	11.17	5.24
Sweden	10.84	16.93	18.01	22.24	10.68	11.67

[a] Data refers to 1999.
[b] Manufacturing refers to the following sectors of NACE Rev. 1: 13-22 and 24-36.
[c] Retail trade refers to the following sectors of NACE Rev. 1: 52.1-52.6 + 50.5.
[d] Transportation and communications refers to the following sectors of NACE Rev. 1: 60-64.

Notes: "Small" refers to enterprises with an annual turnover of less than €7 million; "medium" refers to enterprises with an annual turnover of between €7 million and €40 million.

Source: BACH Database, August 2003.

Trade credit is easily accessible even under conditions of slow growth or recession when banks become more reluctant to lend. The charges involved in this form of financing include the financing cost and a risk premium. Frequently, a cash discount for immediate payment is offered by the supplier, which if not used by the client constitutes an additional cost. Further, many SMEs are not able to pay their suppliers on time before they are paid by their customers owing to liquidity constraints. The same survey confirmed that a large proportion of companies are forced to pay invoices later because they are not able to generate sufficient cash-flow.

---

26 The survey was conducted in 23 European countries in February 2005. More than 6,500 companies took part in the survey.

Not surprisingly, the amounts owed to trade creditors are larger in countries with longer payment periods[27] (Table 10). The effective payment periods differ by country: for example, in 2002, it took on average 87 days before payment was made in Italy (corresponding to a delay of 21 days), whereas in Sweden, firms collect their debts within an average of 34 days (corresponding to a delay of only 8 days). This trend is confirmed by the Intrum Justitia survey (2005), which revealed that invoices in the Nordic countries are generally paid with a delay of one week with respect to the agreed terms, while in southern countries such as Italy and Spain, delays average between two and three weeks – with the notable exception of Portugal, where payments are made up to five weeks after the due date. The same survey in 2005 showed an overall increase of the average payment duration to 57.4 days in 2004 as compared with 56.2 days in 2003.

Table 10. Payment behaviour in Europe in 2001-02 (in days)

	Payment target		**Payment delay**		**Total**		
	2001	2002	2001	2002	2001	2002	2004*
Italy	64	66	24	21	88	87	91.7
Belgium	41	39	20	22	61	61	58.7
France	45	46	12	10	57	56	58.7
UK	29	31	28	23	57	54	51.4
Netherlands	26	26	21	20	47	46	58.7
Germany	23	23	18	17	41	40	41.1
Austria	25	27	13	10	38	37	41.1
Switzerland	24	22	16	14	40	36	41.1
Sweden	24	26	8	8	33	34	31.8

* Data for 2004 from Intrum Justitia (2005).

Source: Creditreform (2003).

Comparing the composition of external financing resources among European countries, no single pattern emerges (Table 11). In Spain, France, Luxembourg, the Netherlands and Portugal, leasing is used more often than overdrafts, while factoring seems to be especially important in France. In other countries such as Denmark, Italy, Ireland and Sweden, enterprises

[27] The payment period is part of the contract between the supplier and client. The difference between the contractual or target payment period and the effective period is the payment delay (late payments). In other words, suppliers offer their customers a payment delay but the latter do not always pay on time; therefore they automatically obtain extra credit.

have a particular preference for using overdrafts to finance their businesses.

Table 11. SMEs' use of external financing in the EU by type (%)

	Overdrafts	Leasing	External investors	Factoring	Bank loans	Subventions
Belgium	37	25	12	4	56	14
Denmark	73	25	13	7	24	7
Germany	47	43	5	2	66	7
Greece	23	15	10	8	68	12
Spain	8	48	15	15	58	10
France	36	47	7	32	63	11
Ireland	70	48	19	14	39	10
Italy	78	41	7	17	17	10
Luxembourg	22	33	15	11	44	15
Netherlands	17	31	11	3	50	9
Austria	42	39	1	6	65	8
Portugal	16	47	7	10	48	6
Finland	46	27	15	14	64	11
Sweden	70	29	10	3	27	6
UK	59	42	11	7	34	10
Total EU-15	50	39	9	11	46	9

Source: Exco, Grant & Thornton survey of SMEs (2001).

Overall, according to the Exco, Grant & Thornton survey of SMEs (2001), 46% of European SMEs rely on bank loans, 50% use overdrafts, 39% use leasing and some 11% use factoring. Hence, the strong reliance on loan finance implies an equally strong need for collateral to secure access to loans for healthy businesses.

1.5 The main constraints to SME financing by banks

Traditionally, SMEs seem to have suffered problems when looking for external financing. For them the cost of borrowing (interest rates and charges) is an important issue. Despite the steady decline of interest rates in the euro area during the past few years, external finance tends to be more expensive for smaller firms than for large ones, as the fixed costs of lending (administrative costs, the cost of collecting information and the risk premium) are not proportional to the size of the loan. [28]

---

[28] See Wagenvoort (2003c).

According to the 2002 ENSR survey, 36% of the respondents were dissatisfied with their banks because they considered the interest rates to be too high, 51% of them thought that bank charges were far too high and 59% were dissatisfied with their bank's services.[29]

Some experts[30] attribute the high lending costs to a lack of competition among lenders in certain regions, which enables them to charge interest rates that are in excess of what the underlying credit risk requires. Small businesses are usually dependent on small local banks, because of their local knowledge and experience, which in turn strengthens the bank-firm relationship and contributes to reducing information asymmetry; but on the other hand, this tends to create market power, allowing a possible extraction of the surplus from SMEs.

To illustrate the financing constraints facing SMEs, the results of a survey undertaken by the European Observatory of SMEs (European Commission, 2003)[31] indicate that about 30% of firms with fewer than 50 employees felt that access to finance was the major constraint to the development of their business (Figure 2).

In terms of the business growth cycle, there are also variations among companies at different points in their development as to how much bank credit is perceived as the main obstacle to their growth (see Table 12).

The availability of bank financing is also contingent on the growth rate of bank lending in relation to the overall business cycle and also to the bank's lending approach.

[29] Efforts have been undertaken, however, by some countries such as Ireland to improve the bank-client relationship. Indeed, the enterprise support unit of the Bank of Ireland introduced a relationship-management approach to the benefit of both the bank and their clients. This approach is complemented by a range of financial and advisory services geared to the particular circumstances of start-ups and developing enterprises, and also includes 'first-step' loans, which are interest-free for a three-year period (European Commission, 2003).

[30] See Berger et al. (1998) for evidence in the US and Schure, Wagenvoort and O'Brien (2004) for evidence in Europe.

[31] The survey covered 7,600 SMEs in 19 European countries (see also European Commission, 2000 and 2002).

Figure 2. Share of firms that consider access to finance to be the major business constraint, by size (%)

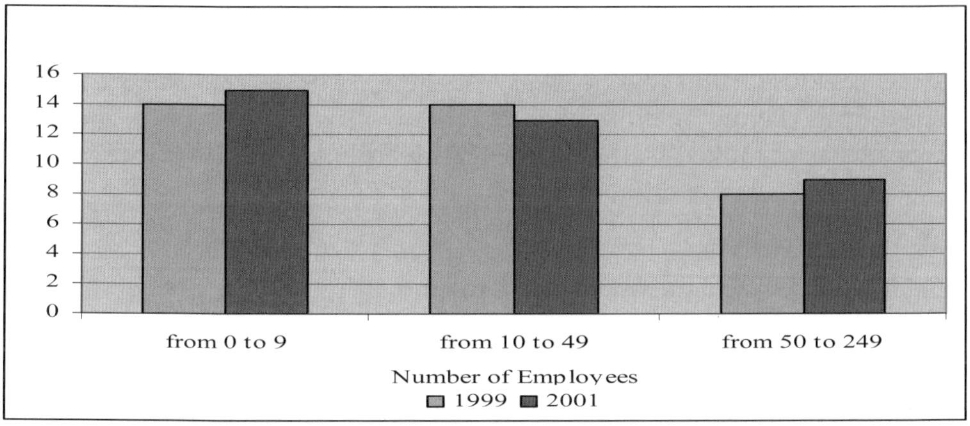

Table 12. Main financial obstacles to growth at the different development stages of companies (%)

Company obstacles	Early stage	Limited growth	Very innovative	Strong growth
Financing as the main obstacle	22	8	16	19
Bank credit	40	40	47	50
Bank guarantees	33	37	44	48
Personal guarantees	25	26	36	39
Guarantees on fixed assets	4	5	5	7

Source: European Commission (2003).

In the past few years, the growth rate of bank lending has slowed – reflecting the weak economic cycle and lower demand as well as more selective lending – to the extent that SMEs have feared a potential 'credit crunch'. This trend was not, however, indicative of banks refusing to grant credit to SMEs, but rather evidence of a more cautious lending approach as banks sought higher profitability and to meet greater risk-management requirements. On the contrary, the EIB survey (2003) of some 70 European banks showed an increase of credit volumes to consumers and businesses during the period 2000-02. Similarly, another survey conducted by

McKinsey & Company for the European Commission (2005c) (hereafter referred to as 'the McKinsey & Co. survey') shows that banks view the SME credit business as a core element of their portfolio and want to increase their growth in this sector.[32]

Looking at the reasons that impede lending to small and medium-sized firms (Figure 3), those banks interviewed by the EIB survey identified four obstacles ranked by their level of relevance:

1) lack of equity in the client's firm,
2) high credit risk,
3) availability of adequate collateral and
4) poor information on the client's firm.

As shown in Figure 3, there are striking differences among the obstacles identified in relation to the development of bank lending to firms of varying sizes. For example, the lack of equity, company risk and available collateral are the main problems for SME financing, whereas low expected profitability is the main brake on financing for large firms. Each of these issues is examined below.

Figure 3. Main obstacles to the development of bank lending to firms

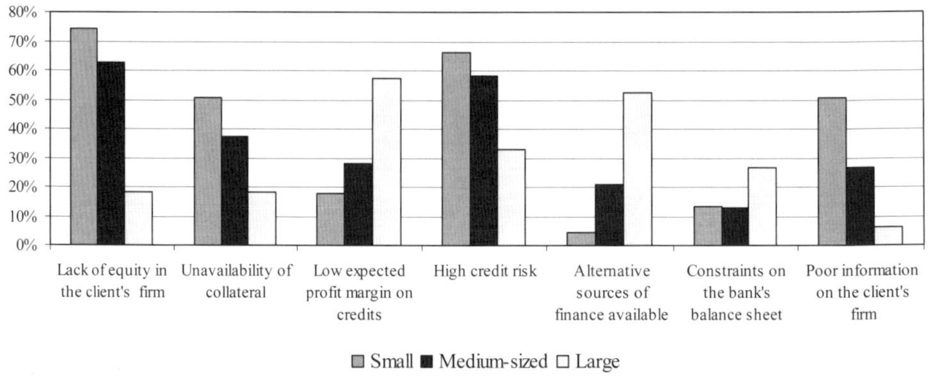

[32] This survey was conducted with a sample of 44 large and 1,000 medium-sized European banks, in which 33 large and 71 small and medium-sized banks responded. The participating banks cover 39% of European banking assets. For more details, see European Commission (2005b).

Lack of equity. As discussed in the previous section, the average rate of equity financing is usually low in Europe, owing to the long-anchored loan financing tradition. The availability of equity in SMEs varies among countries and depends on the SME's size. As previously noted in Table 6, equity shares vary between 13% and 51% in Europe. In France, Belgium and Portugal, for example, equity financing is more prevalent but still it represents one-third of the total balance sheet. This variation is primarily a result of heterogeneous tax laws among the member states, which may be more favourable in some countries such as Belgium[33] and less favourable in others such as Germany.

High credit risk. When launching a new business or an innovative project, the entrepreneur is normally better informed about the project risks than those financing it. This may prevent lenders from observing the real nature of the borrower or influencing the borrower's strategic behaviour after the credit is released. As a result, the lender could voluntarily raise the risk premium on loans (see Annex 1) to properly manage its risks,[34] which translates into higher interest rates for borrowers. This situation may trigger an adverse-selection effect that encourages riskier behaviour owing to the moral hazard principle, which in turn enhances the probability of default and may encourage credit rationing. Indeed, the borrower may suffer from credit rationing as they may not be able to obtain as much credit as they want even though they are willing to pay the interest rate set by their lenders or meet extra conditions to ensure their solvability.[35]

In view of the upcoming regulatory changes for European banks (Basel II and the CRD), the proper management of credit risk will be even more important than it is today. Hence, banks will rely on more sophisticated risk-management techniques and extensive information on

---

[33] It is commonly known that tax regimes in the UK and Ireland are more favourable to the establishment of SMEs, but no data on the average rate of equity financing were available.

[34] Governments in many countries are aware of the negative effect that credit rationing has on SME growth and have undertaken initiatives to address the perceived funding gap in their national economies. These include investing in loans and equity guarantee schemes, venture capital trusts, grants, equity investments and other programmes.

[35] The theoretical literature on credit rationing as a result of asymmetric information was initiated by Stiglitz & Weiss (1981).

the borrower to derive the probabilities of default and other risk parameters.

Availability of adequate collateral. A bank is inclined to ask for collateral to reduce the loan loss in the event of default. For an SME, however, providing collateral is not always an easy task,[36] especially the type that protects the lender for the amount of risk taken.[37] This situation may explain why 23% (and 34%) of those SMEs employing between 0-9 employees and between 10-49 employees respectively are not able to access bank loans according to the ENSR survey (2002).

Informational opacity. Small firms are considered to be more vulnerable than larger ones as they face less rigorous reporting requirements owing to their age and their short credit history. Indeed, unlike larger firms, small firms do not enter into contracts that are publicly visible and widely reported in the press - contracts with their labour force, their suppliers and their customers are generally kept private. In addition, small businesses do not issue traded securities that are continuously priced in public markets. Nor do they have audited financial statements that can be shared with any provider of outside finance. Some family-owned businesses, for example, are very reluctant to report strategic (sometimes considered to be confidential) information such as business structure, growth opportunities, strategic orientation and even ownership structure. As a result, small firms are often unable to convey their status in a credible way, and have more difficulty building a reputation to signal their high quality as a borrower. The inherent characteristics (and weaknesses) of SMEs in terms of size and limited access to capital markets feed their informational opacity, which may prevent easy access to sources of finance and in some cases makes financial contracting problematic.

---

[36] It is necessary to define what kinds of assets are acceptable collateral from the bank's point of view. The most common form of collateral is real estate (either owned by the business or privately owned by the entrepreneur). It may also happen that SMEs assign private or personal savings books to banks as collateral. Other assets such as accounts receivable, inventories or fixed assets could serve as collateral if they fulfil specific conditions.

[37] SMEs generally lack sufficient collateral. Yet even if collateral is available, an economic slowdown may have a negative effect on its value (European Commission, 2001).

According to the Observatory of European SMEs (European Commission, 2003), the availability of information is a basic condition for granting loans to small- and medium-sized enterprises. But the evidence shows that banks only receive balance sheets and the profit and loss accounts from about two-thirds of their SME clients. More sophisticated documents such as budgets for the next few years, financial plans, cash-flow forecasts, information on inventories, unpaid invoices or qualitative information are seldom provided. Generally, the provision of all the information required is a perquisite to extend a loan or an overdraft.

Yet some improvements in the information flow have been observed in comparison with a few years ago. SMEs are becoming more proactive and they more readily deliver their financial statements and inform their banks about major developments in their businesses. Nevertheless, the information provided by SMEs is less sophisticated and less well-structured or validated as compared with the information provided by large enterprises. Small firms usually have small accounting departments or none at all. The entrepreneurs themselves may lack financial administrative skills or are so involved in day-to-day business matters that the documents required by the bank are often neglected. Entrepreneurs should overcome these weaknesses before the implementation of the new CRD in Europe. Indeed, providing balance sheets and profit and loss accounts will be a standard requirement for all enterprises in Europe in order to have access to banking finance.

To explore the list of obstacles to SMEs financing, we conducted direct interviews with banking experts. According to them, the four factors mentioned above are not the only factors that impede the granting of loans. Poor business performance, a lack of entrepreneurial skills and uncertain development prospects are shown to be equally important. The first of these – poor business performance – can be indicated by a low equity ratio, insufficient cash-flow and liquidity problems. The latter two problems can be exacerbated by late payments as well as by bad credit management.

If some of these obstacles are assessed as being prevalent, many banks are not willing to provide or extend a credit line, even if the SME can offer enough collateral. For some existing clients, the reduction of current credit facilities is more likely to happen than a complete withdrawal of all facilities extended to the firm. This reduction is essentially a consequence of the bank's assessment of the risk profile of the firm. The extension of existing credit lines to SMEs might become more difficult as a result of the more stringent regulatory conditions of the new capital requirement rules.

Based on the analysis above, it can be concluded that although alternative financing sources such as leasing, factoring and trade credit exist, SMEs rely heavily on bank financing. But bank financing requires a large volume of financial and strategic information that ought to be provided by SMEs to reduce the information gap between the borrower and its lender. In the face of the new requirements of Basel II globally and the new CRD in the EU, banks will have to reconsider their traditional approaches. Further, the new rules introduce stricter requirements to counter growing concerns about risks at the European and global levels. SMEs need to understand these regulatory changes as they will have some impact on their financing conditions, not necessarily by reducing their credit facilities but by rendering the whole process more risk-sensitive and dependent on the individual quality of the borrowers.

The next section addresses capital regulation in more detail, with an in-depth discussion of Basel II and the CRD.

2. The Basel Capital Accord, the CRD and SME financing

Many questions arise when speaking about capital regulation: What is capital? Why do banks need to hold capital to conduct their business? What is the role of capital in banking? How much capital are banks required to hold? And how do capital requirements for banks impact SME financing conditions?

2.1 Why are banks required to hold regulatory capital?

History has shown the grim reality of a banking industry tainted with worldwide failures and fiascos[38] arising from errors of risk management. Thus, the objective of capital regulation has always been very simple: to reduce the number of bank failures. Sufficient capital must therefore be

[38] For example, not too long ago (in 1995), the UK's oldest merchant bank, Barings, also known as the 'Queen's bank', went bankrupt as a result of the embezzling actions of a single trader based at a small office in Singapore and the incapacity of the risk-management team to avoid the worst consequences. This story is one among several.

maintained to provide a cushion to absorb losses that would otherwise cause the failure of a bank (see Box 2).

Box 2. What is capital in a regulatory context?

In the regulatory context, capital is defined on a two-tiered basis:

- Tier 1 capital (or core capital) includes stock issues (shareholders' equity) and disclosed reserves. Disclosed reserves can be in the form of loan-loss reserves set aside to cushion future losses and smooth out income volatility.
- Tier 2 capital (or supplementary capital) includes perpetual securities, unrealised gains on investment securities, hybrid capital instruments (e.g. mandatory convertibles), long-term subordinated debt with maturity greater than five years and hidden reserves, such as an excess allowance for losses on loans and leases. The total of tier 2 capital is limited to a maximum of 100% of the total of tier 1 capital.

The 1995 proposal of the Basel Committee on Banking Supervision also provided for a third tier of capital consisting of short-term unsecured subordinated debts that can only be used for meeting market-risk capital requirements.

Source: BIS (1988).

Among the risks that a bank must manage, credit risk is fundamentally the most important, particularly when a bank mostly focuses on retail and corporate activities, including lending to small- and medium-sized enterprises. Credit risk is the risk of loss due to the failure of the counterparties to meet their obligations as stated in a loan contract.

A bank must also manage other types of risks, such as market risk when it manages securities and bonds in its balance sheet, and operational risk when it relies heavily on information technology and human resources. By definition, market risk is the risk of loss owing to a change in market prices, such as equity prices, interest or exchange rates. Operational risk is the risk of loss resulting from inadequate or failed internal processes, persons or systems, or from external events.

As a consequence, a bank that manages these risks is required to hold capital, referred to as capital requirements or the capital adequacy ratio, to limit its leverage and provide a buffer against unexpected losses. The retention of sufficient capital decreases the likelihood of a bank becoming insolvent and reduces the negative impact of bank failure through its loss absorption and increased public confidence. Nevertheless, high capital adequacy ratios do not guarantee the bank's soundness, particularly if the risks being taken are high or the bank is mismanaged. Therefore, supervisors consider a bank's capital adequacy in the context of a broader set of factors. But the bottom line is that capital is an important indicator of a bank's general condition and a signal to capital markets, and minimum capital requirements are one of the essential supervisory instruments. In many cases, higher capital requirements could prove necessary for bank loans to higher risk clients - in times of recession, for example, the management of credit risk for these types of loans may turn out to be difficult and undoubtedly the primary source of banks' losses.

2.2 Basel I and its shortcomings

The Basel Capital Accord (Basel I) - the current international framework on capital adequacy - was adopted in 1988 by a group of central banks and other national supervisory authorities working within the Basel Committee on Banking Supervision (BCBS).[39] The 1988 Accord[40] set out details for measuring capital adequacy and the minimum standards for implementation into the national laws of the G-13 member countries by December 1992.

The Basel I Accord has two fundamental objectives, namely:

- to "strengthen the soundness and the stability of the international banking system"[41] by creating common minimum capital adequacy requirements for internationally active banks to set aside a capital cushion for the amount of risk taken; and

---

[39] The BCBS was created in 1975 within the Bank of International Settlements in Basel. The Committee brought together bank supervisors from the G-13 countries (Belgium, Canada, France, Germany, Italy, Japan, Luxembourg, the Netherlands, Spain, Sweden, Switzerland, the UK and the US) to respond to the myriad of bank failures that undermined financial stability in the 1970s. It has no formal authority; rather, its objective is to develop broad supervisory standards and promote best practices, in the expectation that each country will implement the standards in the ways most appropriate to its circumstances. Agreements are developed by consensus, but decisions about which parts of the agreements to implement and how to do so are left to each nation's regulatory authorities.

[40] See BIS (1988).

[41] Ibid.

- to create a level playing field among international banks by establishing that the framework should be fair and consistent in its application to banks in different countries.

The original framework assessed capital mainly in relation to credit risk and addressed other risks (such as market risk, liquidity risk and operational risk) only implicitly - it effectively loaded all regulatory capital requirements into measures of credit risk.

Specifically, the 1988 capital framework requires banks to hold capital known as 'regulatory capital' through the combination of equity, loan-loss reserves, subordinated debts and some other instruments, equal to at least 8% of all the risk-weighted assets (RWA) (such as loans and securities) and asset-equivalent off-balance-sheet exposures (such as loan commitments, standby letters of credit and obligations on derivatives contracts) in their portfolios.[42] This defines a common measure of solvency known as the 'Cooke Ratio' (see Box 3).

The assignment of risk weights is based on the perceived credit quality of an individual obligor and each off-balance-sheet exposure is converted to its equivalent amount of asset and then weighted accordingly. Four broad categories of capital charges are set by the Basel I Accord:

- government exposures with OECD countries receive 0% credit-risk capital charges;
- OECD banks and non-OECD governments receive a 1.6% capital charge (which corresponds to a risk weight of 20%);
- mortgages receive a 4% capital charge (which corresponds to a risk weight of 50%); and
- other remaining exposures such as those to other banks and all corporations including SMEs receive a capital charge of 8% (which corresponds to a risk weight of 100%). More recently, the 1996 amendment[43] to the Basel Capital Accord extended the initial

---

[42] In addition to on-balance-sheet activities, the Basel framework takes into account the credit risk of off-balance-sheet items by applying credit conversion factors to the different types of off-balance-sheet assets, so that they can then be treated as on-balance-sheet items.

[43] Amendment of the Capital Accord to incorporate market risks, BCBS, January 1996 (BIS, 1996).

requirement to include risk-based capital adequacy for market risk in the trading books of the banks.

Box 3. How to calculate minimum capital requirements according to the 1988 Basel Capital Accord

Capital adequacy for on-balance-sheet exposures, as measured by the two-tiered capital regime, will result in a risk-weighted ratio in which the bank's total capital requirements are related to the different categories of on-balance-sheet exposures weighted to the four risk categories displayed in Table B.3.1.

Table B.3.1. Risk weights of on-balance-sheet assets

Risk weights (%)	Asset category
0	Cash and gold held in the bank, obligations on OECD governments and US treasuries
20	Claims on OECD banks, securities issued by US government agencies, claims on municipalities
50	Residential mortgages
100	All other claims: corporate bonds, less-developed countries' debt, claims on non-OECD banks, equity, real estate, plant and equipment, mortgage strips and residuals

The aggregate euro amount in each risk category is then multiplied by the risk weight assigned to that category. The resulting weighted values from each of the risk categories are then added together. The sum is the bank's total risk-weighted assets, which forms the denominator of the Cooke Ratio. Finally, the required capital for the bank must be equal to at least 8% of the total risk-weighted assets in the bank's portfolio. For example:

An unsecured loan of €100 to a non-bank entity requires a risk weight of 100% (Table B.3.1). The risk-weighted asset is therefore:

RWA = €100*100% = €100

A minimum of 8% capital requirement results in 8%*RWA= 8%*€100=€8.

Source: BIS (1988).

Basel I has served its purpose of promoting financial stability and providing an equitable basis for competition among internationally active banks since its inception in 1988. Undoubtedly, throughout the numerous turbulent market events during the past decade (i.e. bank failures such the Barings collapse in 1995), Basel I has provided the needed stability among these banks by strengthening the capital base of the international financial system. Nevertheless, in spite of its success, Basel I was seen to suffer from many shortcomings. Its inadequacy was mainly triggered by major innovations in the banking industry and advances in risk-management techniques, as discussed below.

The *first* limitation of Basel I is related to the overly simplified approach inherent to its architecture. Indeed, as previously explained, the use of only four broad credit risk-weighting categories for capital charges does not provide enough granularity in the measurement or distinction of different levels of credit risk embedded in banking portfolios, especially to address the activities of the most complex organisations. This limited differentiation among degrees of risks means that calculated capital ratios are often uninformative and may provide misleading information about a bank's capital adequacy relative to its real risks. As an example, suppose 'bank A' has a portfolio of different quality borrowers. This bank is required to hold 8% of capital adequacy on its overall portfolio irregardless of the quality of its borrowers, which in turn means that a better quality or investment grade borrower is not rewarded by its bank (with better terms in its loan policy, better rates and more access to loan financing).

Second, the most obvious limitation, which is a result of the limited differentiation among degrees of risks, is the creation of incentives for banks to engage in 'gaming' through regulatory arbitrage provided by asset securitisation and some other innovative financial vehicles including credit derivatives. The general idea behind these new instruments is to allow banks to trade their credit risk exposures in order to transfer the risk to other financial actors in the market. In other words, thanks to these new instruments, banks tend to trade exposures for whatever regulatory capital requirement is higher than what the market requires. As an example, residential mortgages are types of assets that banks securitise in large volume because they believe the required regulatory capital to be greater than market or economic capital (see Box 4). As a consequence, asset securitisation has rendered the 1988 Accord's minimum capital requirements ineffective as a tool to hold capital against the real risk taken. Through asset securitisation, banks have been able to significantly lower their credit risk-based capital requirements without reducing the actual credit risk embedded in their banking portfolios.

Third, a one-size-fits-all approach to risk management is not adequate for banks of different levels of complexity in determining minimum capital requirements, nor does it provide them with enough incentives to improve risk-management techniques. Moreover, the 1988 Accord gives very little attention to credit-risk mitigation. Despite the rapid expansion of credit derivatives as a risk-management tool during the past decade, the current Accord does not recognise offsets on the banking book through credit-risk mitigation techniques covering collateral, guarantees,[44] credit derivatives and on-balance-sheet netting.

Finally, with the exception of the 1996 amendment to extend capital adequacy to market risk, the 1988 Accord focused primarily on credit-risk capital requirements and did not keep pace with banking industry developments. Indeed, over the past 15 years, banks have extensively used the technological advances in information technology to improve their risk-management techniques and functions that cover a far more comprehensive range of risks outside credit and market risks.

Box 4. What is economic capital?

Economic capital is a bank's own estimates of the capital needed to support its risk-taking activities. It represents the emerging best practice for measuring and reporting all kinds of risk across a financial organisation. It is called 'economic' because it measures risk in terms of economic realities. It is called 'capital' because part of the measurement process involves converting a risk distribution to the amount of capital that is required to support the risk, in line with the institution's target financial strength (e.g. credit rating).

An economic capital framework allows banking institutions to drive a return on equity discipline into individual transaction decisions through risk-based pricing. Risk-based pricing can be a key competitive differentiator. Indeed, the banks that use risk-based pricing are able to 'cherry pick' the most profitable loans through aggressive pricing; those not using this technique will accumulate a disproportionate share of under-priced and higher-risk loans.

Leading global banks that have embraced the economic capital framework include: ABN Amro, Deutsche Bank, Bank of Ireland, Barclays, SE Banken and ING.

---

[44] According to a survey of industry views undertaken by the capital group of the BCBS in January 2000, collateral and guarantees are the most widely used credit-risk mitigation techniques.

2.3 Basel II: A new era of risk management

Since 1998, the BCBS has been engaged in a revision process of the 1988 Capital Accord: in 2001, it published the second consultation paper (CP2); in 2003, the third consultation paper (CP3) improved the previous version of the Accord; and in June 2004, the new Basel Capital Accord (Basel II) was formally released.

The application of the new Accord will be gradual from year-end 2006 until year-end 2007. The Committee explicitly stated that the standardised and the IRB approaches for credit risk and the basic and standardised approaches for operational risk remain scheduled for the end of 2006. The advanced IRB approach for credit risk and the advanced measurement approach for operational risk will be deferred until the end of 2007 in order to provide additional time for supervisors and the industry to develop a consistent and reliable method of implementation.

The new Basel Capital Accord introduces an evolutionary and flexible approach to banking supervision, which reflects the rapid progress and sophistication of banking practices and risk-management techniques. By aligning regulation and supervision with these techniques, the new capital framework not only provides strong incentives for banks to continue improving their internal risk-management capabilities but also gives the necessary tools to supervisors to enable them to react to any emerging matter that occurs and thus reduces the regulatory arbitrage opportunities that the existing rules create.

Indeed, Basel II introduces a number of new aspects to the regulation and supervision of banks, structured around three mutually reinforcing pillars:

- pillar 1: minimum capital requirements,
- pillar 2: supervisory review and
- pillar 3: market discipline.

2.3.1 *Pillar 1 – Measuring credit and operational risks for capital requirements*

The computation of the minimum supervisory capital under the first pillar will be based on the sum of the capital requirements originating from: 1) credit risk, 2) market risk and 3) operational risk (see Box 5).

Box 5. The capital ratio under Basel II

Regulatory capital / *risk-weighted assets (measure revised)* = minimum required capital ratio (8% minimum unchanged)

Credit risk exposure (*measure revised***) + market risk exposure (***measure unchanged***)**
+
operational risk exposure (*explicit measure added*)

The main novelties in the first pillar are the variety of approaches for estimating the minimum supervisory capital, which include the standardised approach and the IRB approaches (i.e. the foundation and the advanced IRB approaches). In the standardised approach, the risk weights will be based on a rating that is provided by external credit assessment institutions or other institutions accepted by national supervisors such as export credit agencies. In the IRB approaches, the rating is produced internally by a bank risk-management system.

1. *Measuring credit risk under the standardised approach*

In the standardised approach,[45] the amount of capital required on an unsecured €1 loan to a private firm – now fixed at 8 cents (8% x €1) – could decrease to 1.6 or increase to 12 cents, based on the ratings issued by the so-called 'external credit assessment institution' (ECAI).

A bank will be allowed to use the ratings of more than one ECAI, but some precise rules will prevent any opportunistic ('cherry-picking') behaviour. Thus, banks will not be allowed to choose, for each customer, the rating source assigning the most favourable judgement (thereby reducing the total amount of regulatory capital).

The risk categories broken down by the ECAI will correspond to different risk weights, a process known as 'mapping'.

Better ratings (type AAA-AA) will bring about lower weights in the computation of risk-weighted assets; moreover, as in Basel I, different categories of counterparties (e.g. non-financial firms, states or banks) will receive different sets of coefficients. This is summarised in Table 13, where ratings by Standard and Poor's are used as a sample scale.

---

[45] The description of the standardised and other Basel II approaches has been drawn from Ayadi & Resti (2004).

Table 13. Risk weights in the standardised approach (%)

	AAA	AAA-	AA+	AA	AA-	A+	A	A-	BBB+	BBB	BBB-	BB+	BB	BB-	B+	B	B-	Below	Unrated	Past due
Corporate			20				50				100						150		100	150
Sovereigns			0				20			50				100				150	100	
Banks			20					50						100				150	50	
Banks, based on their country of incorporation			20				50			100				150				150	100	
Retail										75										150
Residential mortgages										35										100
Commercial real estate mortgages										From 100 to 50% according to national supervisors										150

Note: Ratings by Standard and Poor's have been used as a sample scale.

Source: Ayadi & Resti (2004).

Although the table may look complex at first glance, its meaning is quite intuitive:

- Rows indicate the different classes of borrowers identified by Basel II (corporates, sovereign entities, banks, small firms and individuals labelled as 'retail') plus some specific facilities.
- Columns report the various ratings or risk categories that can be assigned to counterparty.

By combining rows and columns, one sees that, for example, a €100 loan to a AAA-rated non-financial company will translate into €20 of risk-weighted assets, and will therefore lead to a capital requirement of 20 x 8% = €1.6 (in other words, 1.6% of the unweighted exposure). Similarly, a €100 facility offered to a sovereign state with a rating lower than B- will give rise to a €150 risk-weighted exposure, hence requiring a capital coverage of 150 x 8% = €12 (12% of the face value).

The last two columns warrant some brief clarification. First, unrated exposures (where no ECAI-issued rating is available) will usually be weighted at 100% (as in the present Accord). This is likely to apply to most European non-financial firms (although some of them will have access to better treatment if included in the retail portfolio, as explained below). Second, past-due loans towards the bank (where a delay of more than 90 days has occurred on any payment) will usually be weighted at 150% (like the worst-rated classes), as payment delays could signal that the borrower is experiencing solvency problems.

2. *Measuring credit risk under the IRB approaches*

If a bank chooses (and is allowed by the national supervisor) to create its own rating system (instead of depending on external agencies), the capital against each credit exposure will be a function of five basic risk parameters:

1. *Probability of default (PD)* is the default probability for a borrower over a one-year period. It is also known as the expected default frequency. A starting point of the measurement of PD is the definition of default. In general, the default event arises from the non-payment of principal or interest. It is commonly admitted that default occurs if payment is past due 90 days. These types of loans are characterised as 'non-performing'.
2. *Loss given default (LGD)* is the expected amount of loss on a facility provided to the borrower when s/he defaults. To determine LGD, a

bank must be able to identify the borrowers who defaulted, the exposures outstanding at the time of default and the amount and timing of repayments ultimately received. In addition, private information on the borrower and the availability of collateral could serve to develop the LGD estimates.

3. *Exposure at default (EAD)* is the amount the borrower owes at the time of default. The EAD is the sum of the current utilisation expressed as a percentage of the total commitment and the loan equivalent, which is the additional utilisation as a percentage of the unused commitment.

4. *Remaining maturity of the exposure* (*m*) raises the possibility that the original probability of default needs to be revised and possibly increased.

5. Finally, there is the *degree of diversification and correlation (rho)* of the credit portfolio to which the exposure belongs.

The expected loss is a simple multiplication of (PD*LGD*EAD). In conjunction with the maturity estimate of the exposure (*m*) and the diversification coefficient (*rho*), these risk parameters are used to determine capital for both economic capital and Basel II regulatory capital models.

Risk weights and thus capital requirements would be determined by a combination of a bank providing the quantitative inputs and the supervisor providing the formulas. The details for calculating capital charges could vary somewhat according to the type of exposure (sovereign, corporate, retail, etc.).

There are two IRB approaches: the foundation and the advanced. The difference between the two is that the former would require the bank to determine only each loan's probability of default and the supervisor would provide the other risk inputs; under the latter, the bank would determine all the risk parameters internally, based on estimations and procedures validated by the supervisor. The choice of operating under either of the two approaches would be required to meet minimum qualifying criteria based on the comprehensiveness and integrity of the banks' internal capabilities for assessing the risk inputs relevant for each approach. Table 14 presents more details on the estimation/computation of the above-mentioned risk factors.

Table 14. Risk factors included in the IRB approaches

Factor	Meaning	Computation in the foundation approach	Computation in the advanced approach
PD	Probability that the borrower is unwilling or unable to pay	The PD must be computed over a one-year risk horizon, accounting for possible deteriorations in the borrower's creditworthiness in the medium to long term.	
LGD	Loss rate in the event of default	The LGD is fixed at 45% for all senior, unsecured exposures. This value must be raised to 75% for subordinated exposures, but can be adjusted downwards **when some recognised collateral is pledged against the loan**. When the collateral is an eligible financial instrument, the LGD can be reduced down to 0%, based on the value of the collateral and on a system of regulatory haircuts. Three types of non-financial collateral are also accepted: receivables, real estate (commercial and residential) and other collateral (including physical capital, but excluding any assets acquired by the bank as a result of a loan default). These non-financial collaterals may drive the LGD down to 40% (35% for receivables and real estate).	Banks will be allowed to use their own estimates of LGDs, provided that they can persuade supervisors that their models are conceptually sound and consistent with their past experience. LGDs will have to be assessed in an economic sense rather than from a mere accounting perspective: when measuring recovery rates, all relevant factors that may reduce the final economic value of the recovered part of the exposure must be taken into account. This includes the discount effect associated with the time elapsed between the emergence of the default and the actual recovery, but also the various direct and indirect administrative costs associated with collecting on the exposure.
EAD	Exposure at default	EAD is computed at 100% of current exposure, plus 75% of undrawn irrevocable commitments. Off-balance sheet exposures will have to be converted into credit equivalents by means of standard credit-conversion factors.	Banks will be allowed to use their own estimates of EAD, provided that they can persuade supervisors that their models are conceptually sound and consistent with their past experience.

Maturity	Time to maturity of the loan	Maturity is conventionally set at two and a half years.	Maturity must be computed as a zero-rate financial duration and will be capped at five years. Maturities shorter than one year will be allowed only in very specific cases.
Correlation	Correlation between the changes in the value of the assets of any two borrowers in the loan portfolio	A rather high correlation (24%) is used for loans to highly-rated, large non-financial firms (the so-called 'corporate' portfolio); this is owing to the fact that such companies are supposed to fail mainly because of systemic shocks (that tend to hit all obligors at the same time). The correlation grows lower (from 24% to 12%) as the borrower's rating worsens: in this case, in fact, idiosyncratic factors are thought to be the main driver behind default risk. The two extreme values seen above (24% and 12%) are scaled down, towards 20% and 8% respectively, when the borrower's turnover is less than €50 million. This is because small firms, too, are supposed to be affected mainly by idiosyncratic risks. Correlations grow even thinner (17% for highly-rated borrowers and 2% for low-rating counterparties) in the case of loans to individuals and small firms included in the 'retail' portfolio. For the so-called 'qualifying revolving-retail exposures' (mainly credit cards and overdrafts issued at a very high interest rate), the correlation coefficients for high and low-quality borrowers range from 11 to 2%. Finally, a fixed correlation of 15% is used in the case of residential mortgages.	

Source: Ayadi & Resti (2004).

3. *Measuring operational risk under pillar 1*

The new capital requirements will not be limited to credit risk: a considerable amount of capital will have to be held against operational risk. Operational risk is defined as "the risk that flaws in a bank's own systems or human resources, as well as external events, may cause unexpected losses, such as those related to mass litigation, fraud or natural catastrophes".[46] To measure operational risk, three approaches are provided by the Accord:

- the basic indicator approach,
- the standardised approach and
- the advanced measurement approaches.

Under the basic indicator approach, banks are required to hold a capital cushion against operational risks equal to 15% of their total gross income (measured as a three-year moving average). This just reflects the fact that larger banks are subject to a higher amount of risk since they are expected to have higher gross income.

Under the standardised approach (note that this is not, in any way, related to the standardised approach to credit risk), the banks' gross income is split among eight business lines: corporate finance, trading and sales, payment and settlement, commercial banking, agency services, retail banking, asset management and retail brokerage. For the first three lines, which are supposed to be more exposed to operational risks, the 15% coefficient is raised to 18%; symmetrically, it is lowered to 12% for the last three lines, which are thought to be less risky.

The advanced measurement approach is designed to be more sensitive to operational risk and is intended for internationally active banks that have significant exposure to operational risk. It seeks to build on banks' rapidly developing internal assessment techniques and would allow banks to use their own methods for assessing their exposures, as long as these methods are judged by supervisors to be sufficiently comprehensive and systematic.

---

46 See BIS (2004).

2.3.2 *Pillar 2 – Supervisory review*

The supervisory review process carried out by national authorities will play a key role under the new Accord in prompting banks to develop, refine and make better use of risk-measurement techniques. This second pillar will translate into four main lines of action. The national regulators will:

- check that the bank's risk-management systems comply with the specifications included in the first pillar of the Accord (such as transparency, integrity and consistency of the internal rating system);
- evaluate risks that fall under the provisions of the first pillar, but which may be imperfectly estimated by its computation formulae (for example the correlation and concentration effects included in the new Accord through a set of standard values may not be appropriate for individual banks);
- assess risks not included under the first pillar (e.g. the interest-rate risk originated by the different maturity mix of assets and liabilities); and
- evaluate how the economic cycle could affect the bank's future capital adequacy. Such effects will have to be estimated though 'stress tests', simulating how the bank's capital requirements would change if a recession were to occur.

In the prudential supervision process, regulators will:

a) verify that each bank has a sound system in place to assess its own capital needs and a sensible strategy to ensure that its capital remains adequate in the future;

b) review and validate such a system, taking appropriate steps whenever it is not fully satisfactory;

c) impose capital requirements above and beyond the regulatory minimum stated in the first pillar if necessary; and

d) act in a quick and timely manner (asking for prompt corrective actions) to prevent the bank's capital from falling below the minimum threshold suggested by its risk profile.

2.3.3 *Pillar 3 – Market discipline*

The third pillar aims at providing the market participants (particularly the bank stakeholders) with all the relevant information that may help them to assess the risk profile of a bank. They will then be able to discipline banks operating with an inadequate capital endowment or an ineffective risk-management system (or both).

Banks are therefore required to release a set of minimum data, both quantitative (e.g. capital adequacy measures and the main aggregates on which capital computation is based) and qualitative (risk-assessment methodologies and related organisational processes). Bank disclosure of the internal rating systems provided for distinct portfolios, including SME portfolios, is generally perceived as a step forward to increase transparency. Nevertheless, the degree of transparency and disclosure is not precisely defined and there is still vast room for manoeuvre. More specifically, nothing is said about disclosing the rating or the criteria used for a specific borrower. The transparency requirements of the third pillar do not apply to any exclusive or confidential information that, if made known to the bank's competitors, could decrease the value of the bank or reduce its competitive advantage.

As a rule, the information required by the third pillar must be released every six months (every year for qualitative data concerning the bank's credit policies, reporting and management systems; every quarter for quantitative data on capital ratios and related aggregates).

2.3.4 *Implementation of Basel II in Europe*

At the European level, the new Basel framework provided substantial background to revise the EU's proposals for the CRD.[47] In July 2004, a proposal for an updated Capital Requirements Directive was published. It mainly kept the same provisions introduced in the Basel II text. Some variations were introduced, however, to accommodate the European context. The new Directive was adopted by the European Parliament on 28 September 2005.

Although originally required to be applied by internationally active banks, the CRD will target all credit institutions and investment firms irrespective of their size, activities or levels of sophistication. The implementation date should follow the same timeframe as that foreseen in

---

[47] Directive 2000/12/EC of 20 March 2000 relating to the taking up and pursuit of the business of credit institutions and Directive 93/6/EEC of 15 March 1993 on the capital adequacy of investment firms and credit institutions (European Commission, 2004b).

the original Basel II framework (i.e. a gradual implementation from 1 January 2007 for the simplest approaches and 1 January 2008 for the most advanced ones).

The scope of application of the new Directive is highly challenging since it should be appropriate for small, medium-sized and large banks as well as investment firms on the grounds that they carry out similar activities and risks. In order to smooth the transition to the new regulatory framework of such a large population of financial institutions varying in size and sophistication, and to make risk-sensitivity achievable by all of them, the Commission has introduced some flexible, European-specific solutions:

- The proposed 'roll-out' rules for the IRB approaches will allow credit institutions to move different business lines and exposure classes to the foundation or the advanced IRB approach during a reasonable timeframe (Art. 85 of the revised Directive).
- Small and medium-sized banks will be allowed partial use of the IRB approaches for some exposures, combined with continued use of the standardised approach for exposures to sovereigns and financial institutions (Art. 89 of the revised Directive).
- Preferential treatment (lower capital charges as compared with the Basel II original text) will be accorded to private equity and venture capital investments when they are considered to be "sufficiently diversified" (Annex VI and Annex VII of the revised Directive).
- Covered bonds will also be given special treatment (Annex VI of the revised Directive).
- Small investment firms will be exempt from the new operational risk charges, reflecting their risk profile and limited systemic importance.

Moreover, to assess the likely impact of these new rules on the European economy, the European Council of Ministers requested[48] the Commission to present a report on the consequences of the Basel II deliberations for all sectors of the European economy with particular attention given to SMEs. In response, the Commission contracted PricewaterhouseCoopers Risk Management in partnership with the National Institute for Economic and Social Research to prepare the study.

---

[48] The request was formulated at the European Council of Ministers meeting in Barcelona on 15-16 March 2002.

The study[49] concluded that the rules would have a positive impact of the new rules on Europe's financial institutions, corporates and SMEs.

For the time being, it is difficult to make an exhaustive evaluation of the effects of the new CRD. But at first glance, a more risk-sensitive calibration and a more obvious linkage between a bank's own risk-management and mitigation techniques along with regulatory capital requirements may provide a natural incentive for banks to implement the most sophisticated tools to manage their risks. Nevertheless, it is important to proceed with a cost-benefit analysis, particularly for small and medium-sized banks that may or may not have the necessary resources to implement such onerous tools. Moreover, if these costs are passed on to consumers and SMEs, their financing conditions may deteriorate and this in turn would adversely impact their growth.

2.3.5 *How do Basel II and the CRD define and treat SMEs?*

Under Basel II and the CRD,[50] SMEs are defined as companies with an annual turnover of less than €50 million. The annual turnover criterion can be substituted by total assets at the discretion of the national supervisor.

Within the SME category, there is an additional distinction between corporate and retail SMEs. First, SMEs are treated in the corporate asset class when the total annual sales are less than €50 million and total exposure to a bank is greater than €1 million. A discount factor that can reach 20% is introduced to correct the asset risk weights on the basis of the borrower's size.[51] Second, SME loans below an exposure size of €1 million can be treated in the retail portfolio[52] (this is subject to a concentration limit and to the requirement that the lending institution actually treats such exposures as retail).[53] The capital requirement in the retail portfolio is less than the corporate portfolio.

---

[49] European Commission (2004a).

[50] See Art. 79 of the new CRD proposals.

[51] The firm-size adjustment factor is an algorithm that modifies the asset correlation in reverse proportion to the SME's size.

[52] Banks considered the retail definition to be arbitrary, rather conservative and unable to reflect how they determine retail and corporate exposures boundaries.

[53] This provision encourages banks to treat as many clients as possible under the retail approach.

At first glance, it is obvious that the definition adopted by the Basel Committee is different from that of the European Commission (2003) as a consequence of the different focus each has had. The Basel II and CRD definition only considers the annual turnover and the size of the exposures, irregardless of the number of employees or the total balance sheet of the SME. What matters is managing the risk of the exposures, which is consistent with the objective of limiting insolvencies in banks' portfolios. The implementation of the CRD in Europe will certainly help to bring about a needed consistency between the two definitions.

Many changes have been undertaken since the beginning of the process,[54] aimed at giving adequate consideration to the capital charges imposed on lending to SMEs under the different approaches of the new Accord. On the one hand these changes have led to a decrease of capital charges on lending to SMEs and on the other hand have provided the possibility of differentiating between SMEs that are part of the retail portfolio and those that are part of the corporate one.[55] Figure 4 shows the change of the slope of the risk weight curve as a function of the probability of default, indicating the more favourable treatment of the SME portfolio, either falling under the lowest part of the corporate portfolio or under the retail one.

---

[54] For example, in the January 2001 consultation paper, the capital charges imposed on the SME portfolio were said to be excessive and could result in hindering their growth.

[55] CEPS carried out a survey on the practical implications of the new Basel II Accord for the European financial system. A questionnaire was distributed to 250 participants at a conference jointly organised by CEPS with FESE (Federation of European Securities Exchanges) and PwC (PricewaterhouseCoopers) on "The Changing Regulatory Regime in Europe: A Challenging New Business Concept" in November 2003 in Brussels. This conference brought together market participants, regulators and academics to discuss the issues raised by the Basel II consultation process almost a month after the Madrid compromise. Accordingly, in order to obtain a direct assessment of how deeply the current proposal has been understood and accepted or even rejected throughout the European financial industry, CEPS undertook a statistical analysis of the 54 relevant responses collected. When asked about the extent to which SME financing had become a political issue, 88% of respondents confirmed the political nature of the SME financing debate and 70% indicated that the agreement on special treatment reached in July 2002 appears rather beneficial (Ayadi & De Rossi, 2004a).

Figure 4. Decrease in risk weights for corporate exposures (LGD 45%; maturity 2.5 years)

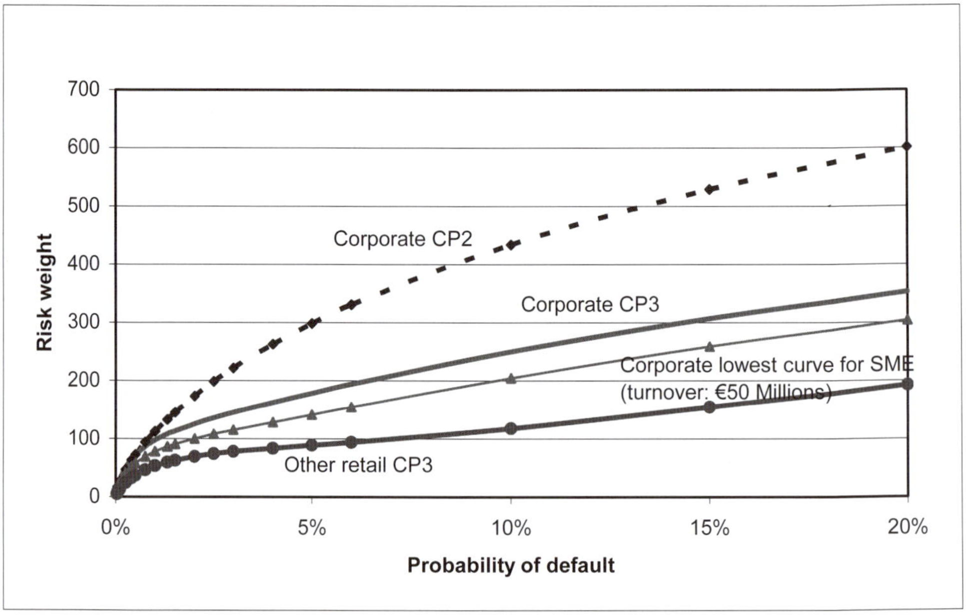

According to the CRD, SMEs will be assessed under the three approaches:

1. For banks that choose to rate their risk exposures *under the standardised approach:*[56]
   - SMEs that are treated as corporate borrowers will receive a risk weight of between 20 and 150%, depending on their rating class quality.[57]
   - Unrated exposures will receive a 100% risk weight, which is equivalent to the current 8% of the unweighted loan.
   - SMEs that are qualified as retail borrowers[58] will receive a 75% risk weight.

---

[56] See Annex VI of the CRD.

[57] As explained previously, the capital charge on a high-quality loan of €100 to an SME rated AAA to AA- is €20 of risk weighted asset multiplied by the original 8% leading to a total of €1.6 (in other words 1.6% of the unweighted exposure). In contrast, a low-quality loan to an SME will give rise to a capital charge of 150 x 8% = €12, which is 12% of the unweighted exposure.

- The treatment of secured loans for SMEs has received particular attention in two cases.
    - o When the loans are secured by commercial real estate, in principle they will receive a risk weight of 100%. Nevertheless, national supervisors will be allowed to assign a reduced risk weight of 50% for 50% of the market value or 60% of the mortgage-lending value when two supervisory tests are fulfilled.[59]
    - o When the loans are secured by mortgages on residential property, they will receive a risk weight of 35%.
    - o Any unsecured exposure will have a risk weight of 100%.
- The treatment of loans that are past due for more than 90 days will receive a risk weight of 150%.
- Finally, exposures associated with investments in venture capital firms and private equity will be assigned a risk weight of 150%.[60] For some cases, national supervisors will apply a risk weight of 50% and 100% to such exposures.

2. *Under the IRB approach,*[61] two alternatives are offered to banks according to whether they use the foundation or the advanced IRB to rate their SME portfolio. Some differences exist depending upon whether the SME is treated as a corporate or as a retail borrower:

    - When an SME is treated as a corporate obligor under the foundation IRB approach, its risk weight depends on the PD, the LGD and the firm size. The LGD for uncollateralised positions is set at 45% and 75% of the loan and is explicitly subordinated.[62]

---

[58] Retail exposures are exposures that comply with the criteria laid down in Art. 79(2) of the Directive proposal 2000/12/EC.

[59] These two tests are: a) the losses resulting from commercial real-estate lending of up to 50% of the market value and 60% of the mortgage-lending value must not exceed 0.3% of the outstanding loans in a given year; and b) overall losses resulting from commercial real-estate lending must not exceed 0.5% of the outstanding loans in a given year.

[60] This is subject to the discretion of competent authorities as per Annex VI, section 11 of the CRD.

[61] See Annex VII of the CRD.

[62] A subordinated loan is a facility that is expressly subordinated to another facility. At national discretion, supervisors may choose to employ a wider

The level of LGD may, however, be reduced to 0% depending on the collateral (eligible financial collateral and receivables, and commercial and residential real estate will receive an LGD of 0% and 35% respectively). The formulas are given in Annex 2.

- Under the advanced approach, the bank is allowed to estimate the risk parameters of an SME exposure. Further, the internal estimates of LGD may lead to lower capital requirements if collateral exists. For uncollateralised positions, the advanced approach may lead to higher capital requirements as the LGD is not limited to 45%. As for EAD and maturity, the internal estimates may vary across banks and lead to higher or lower capital charges.
- When an SME fulfils the qualifying criteria to be treated as a retail exposure, a bank must provide its own estimates of the underlying risk components irrespective of whether it is applying the foundation or the advanced IRB approach. The risk weight depends on the estimates of the PD, LGD and EAD. This would theoretically lead to lowering the capital requirement compared with the risk-weight function for corporates.
- Under the IRB approach,[63] any equity exposure is subject to a set of considerations as outlined below.
    - If a bank is using the simple market-based approach, this will entail risk weights of 190% for private equity exposures in sufficiently diversified portfolios, 290% for exchange-traded equity exposures and 370% for other equity exposures. These risk weights are much lower than those originally applied in the Basel II text.
    - Otherwise, the other approaches (the PD/LGD approach and internal models approach) may trigger more differentiated risk weights depending on the risk type of these exposures. Under the original Basel II framework, these risk charges could not be lower than 200% for firms with publicly traded equities and 300% for those with private equities. For some

definition of subordination. This may include economic subordination, such as in cases where the facility is unsecured and the bulk of the borrower's assets are used to secure other exposures.

[63] See Annex VII, section 1.3 of the CRD.

long-term investments or existing positions, exemptions or transitional arrangements may apply and lead to a risk weight of 100%. All other investments will imply significantly higher capital charges.

2.3.6 *How does the CRD treat collateral?*

Under the CRD proposal, the European Commission has made a distinction between funded and unfunded credit protection.

Funded credit protection refers to a technique of credit-risk mitigation in which the reduction of the credit risk on the exposure of a credit institution derives from the right of the credit institution – in the event of default of the counterparty or on the occurrence of other specified credit events relating to the counterparty – to liquidate, to obtain transfer or appropriation of, to retain certain assets or amounts, to reduce the amount of the exposure to, or to replace it with the amount of the difference between the amount of the exposure and the amount of a claim on the credit institution (Art. 4 §31 of the revised Directive 2000/12/EC). In addition to residential and commercial real estate, all financial items including cash, certificates of deposit or comparable instruments issued by the lending bank, gold, debt securities, some qualified shares and mutual funds investing in the above-mentioned instruments, all listed shares and life insurance policies and other instruments issued by third-party institutions are considered to be eligible collateral under the funded credit protection.

Unfunded credit protection refers to a technique of credit-risk mitigation in which the reduction of credit risk on the exposure of a credit institution derives from the undertaking of a third party to pay an amount in the event of the default of the borrower or on the occurrence of other specified events (Art. 4 §32 of the revised Directive). The eligible providers of unfunded protection are detailed in Annex VIII, part 1 and in Annex VI part 4 of the revised Directive 2000/12/EC.

Under the standardised and IRB foundation approaches, besides residential and commercial real estate, other types of collateral are acceptable, including a wide range of financial collateral. Each type is subject to a different treatment:

1. Under the simple approach, the portion of the exposure covered by recognised collateral receives the risk weight applicable to the

collateral itself, not to the original borrower (usually subject to a floor of 20%).

2. Under the comprehensive approach, no capital requirement is applied to the collateralised portion of the exposure, but the value of the collateral must be trimmed by a fraction (a discount factor), reflecting the risk that the market value of the financial instrument pledged by the borrower may decrease before it is revaluated or remargined.

Guarantees and credit derivatives are considered to be forms of unfunded protection. They are acceptable under the standardised and IRB foundation approaches as credit risk mitigants, provided that they are eligible and fulfil the minimum requirements set in the revised Directive 2000/12/EC (Annex VIII, part 2).

Under the IRB advanced approach, besides the eligible collateral recognised under the standardised and the IRB foundation approaches, other forms of collateral known as eligible IRB collateral are also recognised. These include accounts receivable, specified commercial and residential real estate and other collateral subject to fulfilment of minimum requirements.

The treatment of receivables is a novelty (see Annex 3). The principle is to extend the risk analysis of the borrower's business, industry and the clients with whom the borrower does business. Hence, the bank is able to review the borrower's credit practices to assess their soundness and credibility.[64]

The treatment of guarantees and credit derivatives under the IRB advanced approach closely follows the treatment under the standardised and IRB foundation approaches. Their eligibility and recognition are also subject to the minimum criteria set by the revised Directive 2000/12/EC in Annex VII, part 4.

Credit insurance can be perceived as a type of guarantee. It could be classified as unfunded credit protection and hence could mitigate credit risk. Nevertheless, credit insurance could be recognised in the group of guarantees as long as it fulfils some minimum requirements common to guarantees and credit derivatives and other operational requirements

---

[64] This process could be time-consuming for bankers as it also requires following-up and monitoring the clients of their small borrowers.

relating to risk-management processes to qualify as a credit-risk mitigant. Therefore, this recognition is conditional and the question remains of whether conditional insurance policies can match the requirements of the recognised guarantees. Moreover, this conditionality does not fully consider the credit-enhancement effect of the protection provided by credit insurance.

In practice, this conditionality may limit the recognition of credit insurance under the new banking regulation and gives banking institutions much room for discretion to accept or reject this form of risk mitigation.

2.4 Development of an internal credit rating system

As previously noted, Basel II has introduced a revolutionary approach to risk management, mainly to respond to the criticisms levelled against the current regulatory capital standards. More specifically, the failure of the present capital regime to capture the intrinsic credit risk in the banking business has led to a unanimous determination to rely on internally developed credit-risk models[65] initiated by the industry and monitored by supervisors.

This gives rise to the question of what is considered to be a 'sound' internal credit risk model. This description should be accorded to a system only when it meets the practical needs of the end users (the banks or other financial institutions that provide finance to SMEs) and wins the approval of the regulatory supervisors. Briefly stated, the model should be able to accomplish two important objectives:

- An internal rating model should be able to accurately assess and quantify the intrinsic credit risk embedded in the bank's portfolio. In doing so, it should introduce both quantitative and qualitative measures that facilitate prudential portfolio risk-management.
- Ultimately, it must provide a mechanism that can be used to determine the economic capital requirement of a bank, and the resulting capital allocation framework must be robust enough to be used for risk-adjusted pricing and other strategic purposes.

Figure 5 is a simplified attempt to illustrate the linkages between the essential components of a sound internal credit risk model.

[65] See Crouhy et al. (2001) for a comparison of the current credit risk models.

Figure 5: Essential components of a sound internal credit risk model

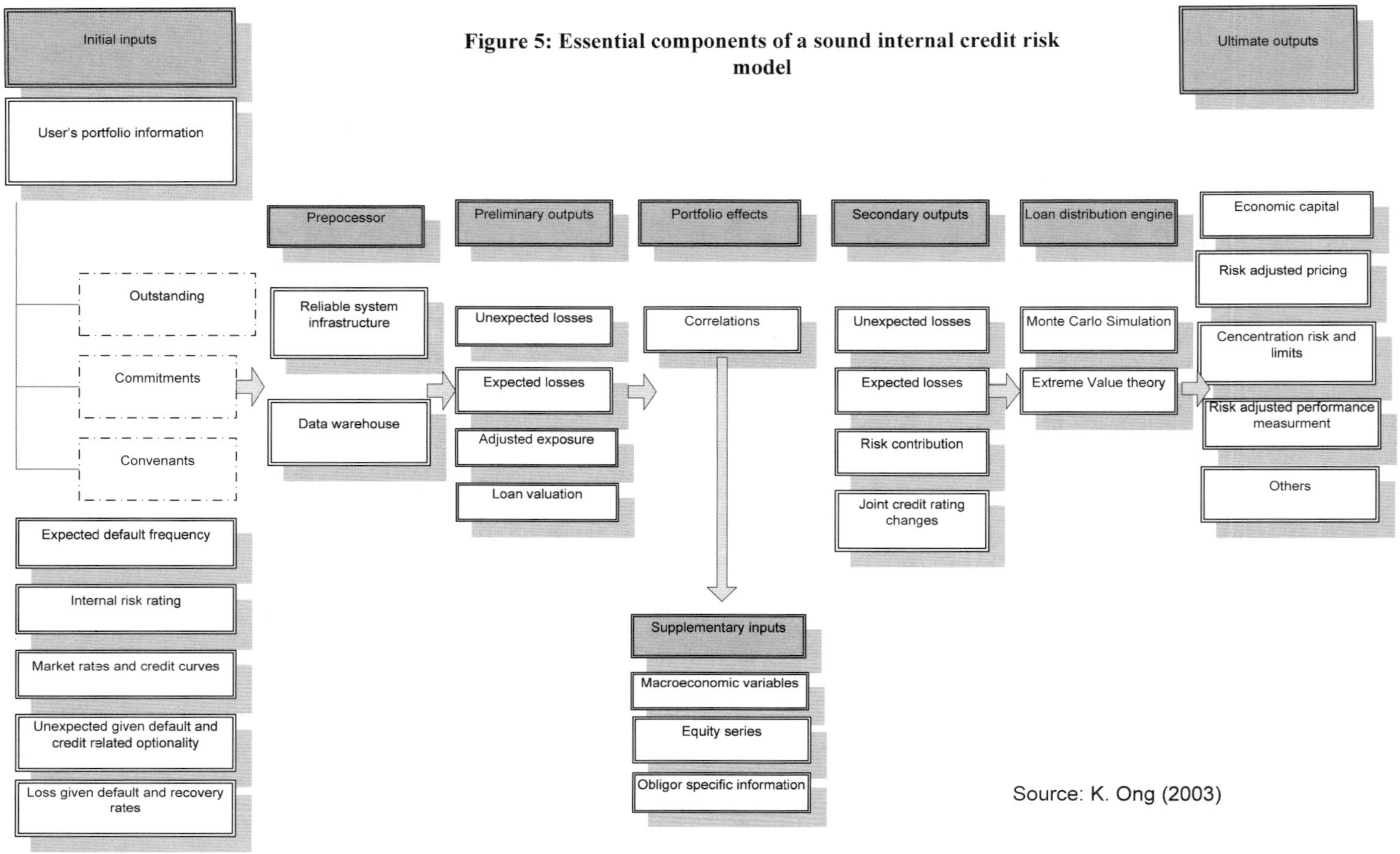

Source: K. Ong (2003)

Clearly, the initial inputs to the model are crucial. For the most part, these are highly dependent on the existing system infrastructure and data warehousing within a bank. The ability to extract customer-related information and current market rates on demand is vital. As an initial benchmark for assessing the creditworthiness of an obligor, the bank's own risk-rating system must be sufficiently robust and granular to distinguish the different levels of credit quality. Other inputs required are the obligor-specific information, such as the probabilities of defaults, recovery rates (or loss-given defaults), outstanding accounts, commitments and covenants.

The next component of the model is the ability to calculate individual risk measurements, for example, expected loss, unexpected loss, adjusted exposure and the marked-to-market valuation of the underlying loan. Subsequently, given supplementary information such as macroeconomic variables, default correlation, sovereign-related quantities and other obligor-specific information, aggregate risk measures can be calculated on a portfolio basis. In order to attach a statistical confidence level to the capital required as a buffer against insolvency, the bank needs to use tools such as the Monte Carlo simulation[66] and extreme value theory[67] to arrive at a desired loss distribution for the portfolio. This leads to the ultimate outputs of the internal model such as risk-adjusted performance measurements, risk-adjusted pricing and economic capital requirements.

Over the last two decades credit-rating models have allowed banks and other financial institutions to assess the risks incurred in their lending activities to SMEs more accurately. Indeed, rating models involve processing data about the firm and its owner using statistical models. The outcome of the whole process is a rating or a set of summary statistics about the borrower's expected future loan performance.

A note of caution, however, is that credit rating is not a 'plug-and-play' approach in which one just inputs data into a computer and uses the

---

[66] The Monte Carlo simulation is an analytical technique for solving a problem by performing a large number of trial runs (i.e. simulations) and inferring a solution from the collective results. It is a method for calculating the probability distribution of possible outcomes.

[67] Extreme value theory is a branch of statistics dealing with the extreme deviations from the median of probability distributions. The general theory sets out to assess the type of probability distributions generated by processes. Extreme value theory is important for assessing risk for highly unusual events, such as 100-year floods.

output at its face value. It requires a major investment in time, technology, training and human resources. Financial institutions have the choice to either develop their own internal credit rating system or to share external rating solutions by pooling data. The pooling of data allows for the creation of a data source that is large enough to undertake historical analysis and enables lenders to benefit from tools that would otherwise not have been available. One classic example is the use of credit bureau data to create pooled risk ratings.

We next focus on the development stages of an internal rating (or scoring) model, since banks that choose to apply the IRB approach will have to implement their own internal models *to assess credit risks*.

First however, we review the system components associated with loans to SMEs.

2.4.1 *Recap of the main risk components of a loan to SMEs*

It is important for SMEs to understand the process followed by banks in assessing credit risk in order to be able to transmit the detailed information that banks need to evaluate their creditworthiness. When using the IRB approaches, banks consider the following components:

1. PD - probability of default by the borrower;
2. EAD - outstanding part of the loan (still to be repaid, hence outstanding risk) or exposure at default;
3. LGD - probability that the financial institution does not succeed in recovering the debt once default has occurred; and
4. M - maturity of the loan.

Capital requirements are computed according to predetermined and simple formulas based on the four components of risks.[68] The main principle of the internal rating is that the financial institution is able to cover expected losses[69] (EL) with the provisions and unexpected losses (UL)[70] with its own capital. Basically, capital requirements address the unexpected losses, which must be fully covered by a bank's lending rates. Expected losses, however, are treated as a cost and not as a risk, and are computed by multiplying the PD, the LGD and the EAD.

---

[68] Refer to Annex 2.

[69] Expected loss is a mean of the future losses.

[70] These losses may or may not materialise for many years.

As already seen, Basel II presents two IRB approaches:

- Under the foundation IRB approach, the rating is focused on the estimation of PD, that is, the probability that a company does not repay.
- Under the advanced IRB approach, besides estimating the PD, the rating takes also EAD and LGD into account.

Probability of default is the most important component of credit risk. It is essential to the two approaches foreseen by both Basel II and the CRD and is therefore the main determinant of capital reserves. The risk elements interact as shown in Figure 6:

- An SME can have a PD within a category or a class, for instance, between 0.01% and 10%.
- The EAD will range in general between 50% and 100% of the loan. Default often occurs soon after lending. The lower the outstanding loan, the less frequently default occurs.
- LGD most commonly fluctuates between 20% and 100%. The worst scenario is that the bank/financial institution does not recover any of the defaulted amounts, and hence, the recovery rate is 0 and the LGD is 100%. In the best scenario, recovery rate will reach 80% of the principal outstanding; hence the LGD will be reduced to 20%.

Figure 6. Interaction of the three elements of risk

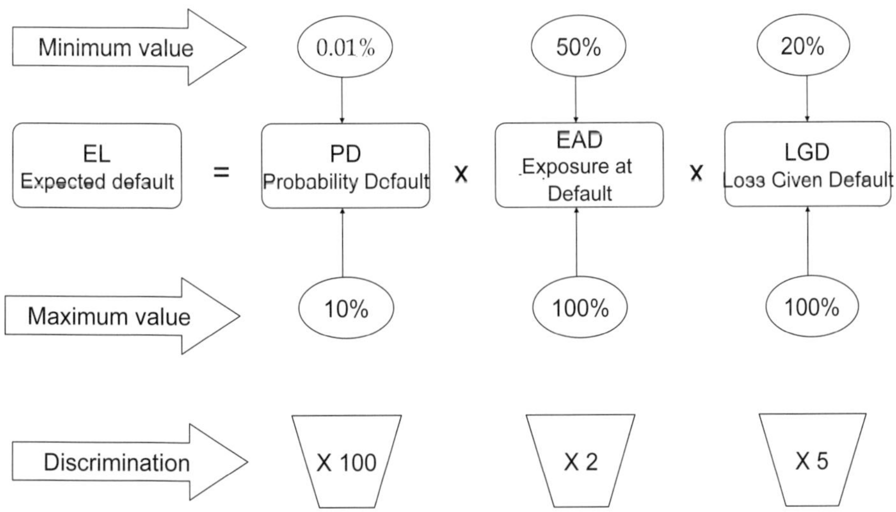

Source: Mercer Oliver Wyman (2004).

The effect of these elements in the capital requirement is the following:

- PD can multiply a given capital requirement by 100.
- EAD can multiply a given capital requirement by 2.
- LGD can multiply a given capital requirement by 5.

Thus PD is also the most determinant factor for calculating capital requirements.

Rating an SME consists of applying a statistical system that multiplies a series of descriptive ratios by a set of coefficients, which results in a certain value (a rating or score). This value allows for comparison between SMEs, establishing a sort of risk gradient: the higher the value is, the higher the probability of default. The value corresponds to a determined risk category, and this risk category is associated with a PD. Therefore, to analyse the impact of a certain rating system, we must look at the ratios used.

To illustrate this, the external rating agencies provide a matrix with the gradual classification of risks. Each rating corresponds implicitly to a PD. As previously discussed, the risk mapping is used directly under the standardised approach (Table 15), whereas under the IRB approaches, PD and the other risk components are estimated internally.

Table 15. Ratings and corresponding PDs

Ratings (S&P)	PD (in %)
AAA	0.01
AA+	0.02
AA	0.03
AA-	0.04
A+	0.05
A	0.07
A-	0.09
BBB+	0.13
BBB	0.18
BBB-	0.32
BB+	0.53
BB	0.93
BB-	1.57
B+	2.64
B	4.46
B-	7.52

Source: Soley Sans & Rahnema (2004).

2.4.2 *Other key elements and the development phases of an internal credit rating system*

The use of data to run objective quantitative and statistical models to evaluate credit risk is commonly known as either a credit rating system or a credit scoring model.[71] The outcome of this automated process is a rating or a score that will assist the decision-making process.

A credit rating model applies different weights to the characteristics used to predict the performance. The weights (or values) measure the influence of that characteristic on the outcome. The weights and the levels of influence are determined by statistical analysis. Only those characteristics that exert a significant influence will be included in the final model. The outcome or performance is the business metric to be evaluated in order to improve the decision-making process; the score or rating assigned to any application is the sum of the appropriate weights given by the values of each characteristic included in the model.

In order to perform well, research points to several characteristics that are essential for rating systems. They must be:

- understandable – the rating system must be easy to verbalise and should be understandable not only statistically but also in business terms;
- powerful – the system must be able to discern clearly between good and bad payers;
- weighted up by default probability – the system must be able to indicate the probability that an individual client could become a bad payer; and
- empirically valid – the system must have shown its predictive capacity.

Rating systems take into account different types of information concerning SMEs. Complete rating systems have three modules.

1) The first module is comprised of economic and financial information on the firm from corporate accounts (balance sheets as well as profit and loss accounts). This information is normally available for the majority of firms. The economic and financial data must be credible

---

[71] Rating models are used when rating small, medium-sized and large enterprises; scoring models are generally used to score individuals.

and reliable (the companies must be audited by reliable auditing institutions).

2) The second module is constructed upon the qualitative data of the enterprise, such as its management, internal processes and human capital base. This data is often gathered on the company's premises.

3) The third module involves an analysis of a bank's proprietary information on the borrower (Figure 7).

Figure 7. Information considered in a rating

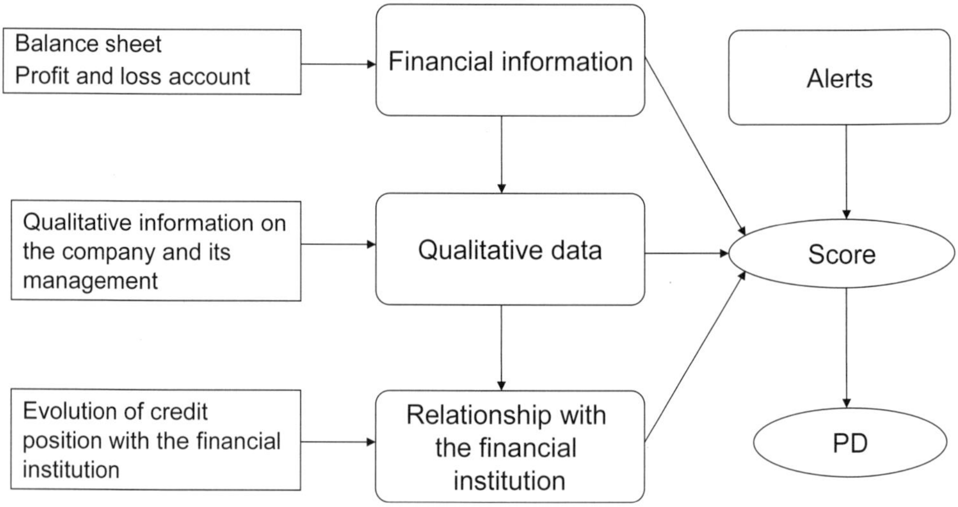

Source: Soley Sans & Rahnema (2004).

Apart from the different types of information used in the construction of rating modules mentioned above, there are other risk indicators or 'alerts' reflecting the historical behaviour of a company when operating with financial institutions (past due loans). This information could be financial, reflecting the solvency history of the company and also qualitative, such as the age of the company or the behaviour of the owner towards the employees. The related information could be collected from private credit bureaus, public credit registries, central banks, judicial archives on the company (and often the individuals), bankruptcy files and other public or private sources available in the different countries.

Some of the information gathered is used to approximate the PD. Other data play a decisive role in the estimation of the level of exposure of the firm (EAD) and severity (LGD) associated with the recovery rate, such as the availability of physical or financial collateral, or guarantees from banks, credit insurance or the principal owner, affiliates or parent firms.

If a default occurs, the estimation of the LGD and EAD are computed by a separate rating model generally used at the origination of the loan. This rating model serves to re-evaluate the collateral and guaranties to allow the calculation of the recovery rate when the default occurs.

Four different stages can be identified in the elaboration of a rating associated with a PD:

1) the gathering of historical information,
2) analysis of individual factors,
3) specification and estimation of the model and
4) verification of PD accuracy.

Phase 1. Collection of historical information

First the rating system of the bank needs to identify the financial and economic profile of the firm from the inception of historical data (year 1, year 2, etc.). These data are either bank-held information or obtained through the national central bank of each country, private external credit bureaus, etc. The rating system needs to reflect the evolution of the credit liabilities of the firm. More specifically, was the company able to repay debt? Did any problems arise that caused default? See Figure 8.

Figure 8. Compilation of historical data

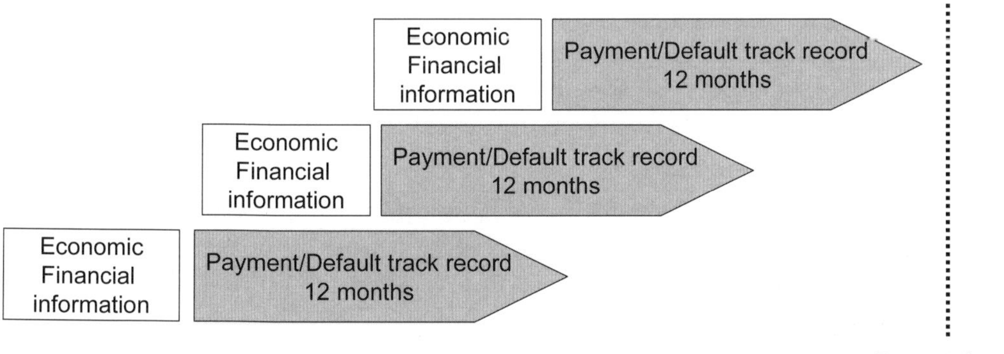

Source: Soley Sans & Rahnema (2004).

The information collected allows for the calculation of predictive ratios that reflect the criteria below, linked to the type of data (qualitative and quantitative).

Quantitative data

- Performance (i.e. the result of ordinary activities/total assets and cash-flow generation)
  - ➢ The higher and the steadier these ratios are, the better the rating and the lower the probability of default. This is an indication of the capacity of the company to generate returns and therefore to meet its credit obligations.
- Leverage (i.e. own capital or equity and total debt)
  - ➢ The higher this ratio is, the better the rating and the lower the probability of default. A higher equity ratio reflects a stronger balance sheet.
- Debt coverage (i.e. net profit plus non-cash expenses/short-term debt)
  - ➢ The higher this ratio is, the better the rating and the lower the probability of default. This is an indication of the capacity of the company to pay short-term debt interest.
- Liquidity (i.e. cash/short-term debt or cash/total assets or accounts payable/total assets)
  - ➢ The higher this ratio is, the better the rating and the lower the probability of default, as this shows that the company has sufficient liquidity to absorb short-term debt.
- Growth (i.e. sales growth)
  - ➢ The steadier sales growth is, the better the rating and the lower the probability of default. A sustainable growth in sales is an indication of the future prosperity of the company.
- Productivity (i.e. sales/assets)
  - ➢ The higher this ratio is, the better the rating and the lower the probability of default. This ratio indicates the capacity of the company to generate sales from the employment of its assets.
- Size (i.e. annual total assets and annual total turnover)

  - ➢ Total assets/total turnover indicate how large the company is and to which bracket it belongs in the bank's assets (corporate versus retail portfolio).

- Other factors such as market conditions, particularly when firms have operations in emerging markets, past due loans, credit history, debt structure, the level of activity diversification, innovation capacity, the level of outstanding trade credit and merchandise disputes with suppliers/clients, etc.
- Macroeconomic factors (e.g. sovereign risk of the country where firms are located, export growth and commodity price levels)

Qualitative data

- Development prospects of the industry
- Availability of a clear, well-structured and credible business plan
- Profile of the enterprise (activity sector, age, growth cycle, number of employees, etc.)
- Capacity/experience, reputation and past credit history of the entrepreneur/manager/owner
- Ownership and governance structure of the firm (the number of shareholders, the distribution of the shares, etc.)
- Management quality of accounts receivable
- Availability of collateral, guarantees, etc. This is a particularly important factor for a bank when it establishes a price for a loan. Providing valuable collateral helps to reduce the interest charges. Even if the rating is poor, providing collateral may help to obtain a loan with less stringent conditions.

The validity of the data set constructed should fulfil three basic premises:

- coverage of a complete economic cycle – data collected must refer to different periods in time covering up to 10 years;
- sufficient quality of information – the ratios calculated must take into account a sufficient number of companies (ratios based upon a small number of companies must be disregarded); and
- data must be representative of the type of enterprise covered – models based on a certain typology of firms are not necessarily applicable to all firms of all types.

To check the validity of these criteria and to complement the list of quantitative and qualitative information needed for the purpose of this study, we sent a qualitative questionnaire[72] to credit risk managers, compliance and auditing experts in some 150 banking institutions located throughout Europe. The questions mainly sought more information about the internal rating systems used by European banks. The banks were selected from a representative sample within the EU-15 plus some Eastern European countries.[73] The sample included at least three lending institutions in different geographical areas. When possible, telephone contact was made with key persons within the bank to explain the purpose of the research. If they agreed to participate, very specific questions were posed through e-mail or follow-up telephone interviews to explore particular issues that either were not well understood or not identified in the questionnaire.

Eight credit risk experts from eight banking institutions participated,[74] geographically distributed as follows Denmark (2), France (2), Portugal (1), Germany (1), Finland (1) and Greece (1) along with two rating experts from two international rating agencies. Among these, three banks intend to comply with the partial use of the IRB approach and the other five are in the process of implementing the IRB approaches (four are in the process of applying the foundation approach and one the advanced approach). The eight banks consider SME lending as either very important to their business (between 20 and 40% of their assets) or the predominant

---

[72] The questionnaire is reproduced in Annex 4. The intention of the questionnaire was to obtain information on the preparations made by banks to comply with the provisions of Basel II related to internal processes for managing credit risk.

[73] The Eastern European countries included Poland, the Czech Republic, Hungary and the Slovak Republic.

[74] Many reasons could explain the low rate of responses. First, some credit managers and/or experts were not prepared to give any responses on the internal rating system they used to manage credit risk. Second, some did not want to disclose aspects of their credit risk-management methods, noting this as confidential strategic information or stating that they would need the agreement of their board to discuss it. Third, some are not planning to adopt the IRB approaches for credit and operational risks. Finally, it should be noted that 15 questionnaires were sent back because the contact person was no longer working in the bank. The low rate of responses does not, however, affect the quality of the results as it is a qualitative survey.

sector (more than 40% of their total assets). The majority consider that at least 20% of their overall SME exposures fulfil the requirements to be qualified as part of their retail portfolio.

They indicated that the historical data they collect are based on easily gathered financial information from balance-sheet statements and profit-and-loss accounts, mostly related to the factors mentioned above. Specifically, data are gathered with regard to the debt/capital structure, the ability of the SME to satisfy its credit obligations through the ratios concerning free cash-flow earnings before interest and taxes, the profit and loss structure and the business plan. These data are determinant when selecting potential borrowers.

They added that the main *qualitative* factors taken into account are those related to the ownership structure, the legal form and the age of the enterprise, the managerial capabilities and reputation of the entrepreneur or owner (experience, age, creditworthiness and his/her share in the capital structure). To obtain this information, the respondent banks prefer to collect it directly from their customers and in some cases from private, external credit bureaus or public credit registries.

The majority of the respondents mentioned the relevance of collateral and guarantees in the process of credit approval, notably when granting medium- to long-term credit. For example, when the collateral is very liquid such as cash or some types of debt securities, the pricing of the loan is lower since the bank is able to recover loan losses if default occurs. Other collateral such as real estate (commercial and residential) and receivables reduce the risk inherent in the loan but necessitate extensive assessment when the borrower defaults. Therefore, the recovery rates would vary depending on the loss given default (LGD) assigned to each loan.

In general, collateral allows an extension of the credit line in terms of volume and duration and in some cases lowers the cost of credit. In particular, when the loan is pledged by accounts receivable, the respondent banks consider that well-managed accounts are far better perceived than those poorly managed. Credit insurance was mentioned by a few responding banks as a valuable guarantee on accounts receivable (or indemnification against default) and also in case the enterprise has operations in emerging markets where political risk may be a factor. It is also said to be a complete risk-management tool that helps management to put in place the necessary procedures to prevent and minimise late payments and defaults, thereby reducing the exposure of the receivables portfolio and enhancing the capacity of using commercial credit as a competitive tool.

Phase 2. Analysis of individual factors

The objective of this stage is to determine which ratios best serve the construction of the final model. The relationship between each of the ratios and the dependent variable (default) and their predictive capacity must be analysed. Those factors offering a low predictive capacity must be excluded from the analysis, along with ratios presenting counterintuitive relations with default.

Phase 2 is mainly a statistical exercise. It depends greatly on the activity sector of companies, their growth cycle and the overall business environment of the company.

When asking the banking experts about the characteristics of this selection phase, they confirmed that it is done through statistical analysis of individual factors and ratios, which are selected according to their relevance in the decision-making procedure.

Phase 3. Specification and estimation of the model

The next stage is to carry out a multivariance analysis to assign weightings to the model, taking into account not only the individual predictive capacity (univariance) of each ratio, but also its co-relationship with other types of information. Other variables are introduced during this phase such as the diversification and the granularity of the portfolio. Phase 3 is essentially an econometric exercise.

Phase 4. Obtaining the rating and the associated PD

Once the model and weightings of the applicable ratios are set, the next stage seeks to systematise the assignment of the PD from the rating obtained through internal statistical models. The establishment of groups of percentiles that will define the rating of a company follows the ordering of enterprises according to their rating. For each rating level, a PD is obtained by observing the proportion of defaulted and non-defaulted companies that obtained that rating in the past.

Responses by bank experts to questions concerning phases 3 and 4 were very divergent, as some were advanced in the PD generation process and others were preparing to establish the best systems corresponding to their businesses. Such divergence was expected, given the efforts underway to get ready for the new rating processes required by the Basel II and CRD regulations.

Finally, depending on the bank or financial institution, the rating is updated every year, sometimes every quarter or month according to some risk managers. If the same conditions are maintained, the assigned rating is stable. If conditions improve (worsen), the rating will also improve (worsen).

The respondent banks indicated that the main factors leading to credit downgrading are:

- the delayed submission of financial data;
- incomplete, unstructured or unclear financial data;
- a worsening of the business and financial factors of the company, such as loss of market share, decreased or negative earnings before interest and taxes, an increase in balance-sheet mismatches (long-term commitments versus short-term liquidity), deterioration of liquidity, an increase of long-term debt, reduced equity ratio, recurring overspends, poor credit management within the company (more late and defaulted payers) and a rise in merchandise disputes with suppliers/clients;
- drastic changes in the ownership structure of the firm, such as the mortality of the owner/manager and absence of future plans or the loss of other key persons; and
- some macroeconomic factors such as an increase in the political risks where the company is located or a reduction of exports.

They also mentioned that they look at excessive overdraft behaviour and blocked payments.

2.4.3 *A rating system in practice*

Rating systems are based on very objective mathematical and statistical systems that render the financing decisions more realistic for the particular situation of a given firm. In practice, a rating system consists of:

- a mathematical formula that assigns a rating (or score) to a company based on a set of ratios; and

- a correspondence to a risk group based on prior ratings and the present quality of the borrower, and finally the assignment of a PD.[75]

A practical example of a credit rating system is RISKCALCTm, a predetermined rating system produced by Moody's KMV to accurately characterise the credit risk of private companies for faster underwriting decisions and providing efficient monitoring of portfolio credit trends. Using this system, we first describe the financial ratios that should be taken into account in the credit risk assessment exercise to produce the desired rating and the correspondent probability of default. Then we show the results given by the RISKCALCTm and offer some explanations based on different circumstances.

The ratios that are weighted in the RISKCALCTm rating system are the following:

- Leverage ratios
    - Own capital/debt – this is a measure of the level of non-distributed profits relative to the total debt.
    - Total debt/total assets – this is a measure to compare the level of debt relative to assets.

The higher this ratio is, the higher the probability of default.

- Liquidity ratio (more specifically, cash/short-term debt) – the higher this ratio is, the lower the probability of default.
- Performance ratio (the result of ordinary activities/assets) – the higher this ratio is the lower the probability of default.
- Debt coverage ratios
    - Net profit plus non-cash expenses/short-term debt – the higher this ratio is, the lower the probability of default.
    - Cash flow/financial expenses – the higher this ratio is, the lower the probability of default.
    - Financial expenses/net sales – the higher this ratio is the lower the probability of default.
- Growth (sales growth) – this is calculated between N and N-1; increased growth implies a lower probability of default.

---

[75] See Soley Sans & Rahnema (2004).

- Productivity (sales/assets) – the higher this ratio is, the lower the probability of default.

The results of a simulation exercise of the data of some companies are reported in Table 16.

The quality of the firms depends on the assigned rating and the correspondent probability of default. Each factor (input) is weighted according to its degree of importance. These weights may vary depending on the models used. The final result improves with the rating and the lower probability of default, revealing how easy it would be for the firm to obtain financing.

For example, firm A has the best rating (AA3) associated with the lowest probability of default. It has the highest own capital/debts, liquidity, cash-flow/debt and cash-flow/financial expenses ratios in comparison with the other firms. On the opposite side of the table, firm K has the worst rating (B3) associated with a high probability of default (26%); this firm has low chances of obtaining a loan with good conditions since it is considered to be highly risky.

These results are mainly based on the economic and financial data collected either directly or through some private credit bureaus or national credit registries. The ratings, however, may also depend on other information that may serve as alerts such as past due loans - for example, in the case of firm G, data collected from a private credit bureau showed that this company has a previous default history with other financial institutions, prior to the rating exercise performed by RISKCALC™. The alert resulted in a downgrade of the company in question irregardless of its current economic and financial situation.

It is important to note that historical data on the solvency of companies[76] can serve as effective warnings that impact their actual and future financing. Other situations such as the loss of a key person in the firm, the loss of market shares, late payments from clients or low innovation capacity can cause the downgrading of the firm. These factors were confirmed by the majority of the banking experts who participated in the survey.

---

[76] This data can be collected in the national credit registries, the judicial archives and in the central banks in each country.

*Table 16. The calculation of an internal rating according to the rating system RISKCALC^Tm^*

	Firm A	Firm B	Firm C	Firm D	Firm E	Firm F	Firm G	Firm H	Firm I	Firm J	Firm K
Own capital/debts	4.155	2.69	1.018	0.262	0.515	0.557	0.942	0.074	0.088	0.125	-1.689
Debt/asset	-0.417	0.122	0.253	0.134	0.612	0.302	0.505	0.779	0.584	0.789	0.867
Liquidity	3.425	0.526	0.998	2437	0.003	0.5	0.01	0.252	0.211	0.048	0.251
Result of ordinary activities/assets	0.081	0.067	0.097	0.071	0.149	0.038	0.067	0.106	-0.016	0.02	-0.338
Cash flow/debt	1.079	0.887	0.546	0.835	0.297	0.112	0.18	0.135	0.216	0.065	0.297
Cash flow/financial expenses	157	-	11.677	6.709	25.952	1.096	5.226	6.276	2.062	2.216	-5.019
Financial expenses/sales	0.001	0	0.022	0.029	0.014	0.038	0.028	0.03	0.038	0.042	0.138
Sales/assets	1.259	0.732	0.949	0.402	0.501	1.309	0.639	0.635	1.831	0.576	0.384
Sales growth	-0.073	0.121	0.085	-0.229	0.04	0.102	0.096	0.809	-0.186	0.13	-0.323
Rating	AA3	A1	A2	A3	BAA1	BAA2	BAA3	BA1	BA2	BA3	B3
Probability of default (for one year) (%)	0.53	0.73	0.87	0.99	1.25	2.24	3.76	4.50	8.12	10.90	26

Source: Example extracted from Soley Sans & Rahnema (2004).

In this practical example, the provision of collateral and guarantees was not included.

At a further stage, the estimation of the probability of default will permit the calculation of the regulatory capital necessary to cover the risk carried in the portfolio of the bank or the financial institution. The higher the probability of default, the higher are the associated capital requirements and the poorer are the conditions for obtaining a loan.

Firm A would receive a loan with very good conditions, whereas firm K would obtain a loan with more stringent conditions to account for the amount of risk the bank would be taking to offer the finance.

2.4.4 *The risk premium: The key component of the cost of credit*

As explained in the previous section, the risk premium depends on three components: the probability of default, the loss given default and the exposure at default.

- The estimation of PD is given by the internal rating, which depends on the economic and financial situation of the borrower and previous solvency history.
- The LGD is the estimation of the percentage of losses over the exposure minus its recovered part and associated costs. LGD depends on the guarantees and collateral provided by the borrowers, which are used to calculate the recovery rate. During interviews with a rating expert from an international rating agency and with a credit risk expert within a bank, they both mentioned that the use of guarantees and collateral are taken into consideration when calculating the recovery rates.
- EAD is the estimation of the amount used by the borrower at the time when she or he defaults. EAD is the sum of the amount of the loan used and a fraction (K) of the available loan. This fraction depends on the type of product and the rating of the borrower.

A good estimation of the risk premium depends greatly on the accuracy of the client rating process. This process will allow their classification according to their creditworthiness by assigning a rating and a PD (see Figure 9).

Moreover, rating is the key element for banks and other financial institutions to determine the return adjusted to risk. Indeed, a growing number of financial institutions have been using risk-adjusted performance measures to measure their economic capital including:

- the return on risk-adjusted capital (RORAC); and
- the risk-adjusted return on risk-adjusted capital (RARORAC) also called 'risk-adjusted return on capital' (RAROC).

In RAROC, the risk-adjusted return is the difference between financial revenues and financial costs minus the potential expected losses and the administrative costs. The risk-adjusted capital is the economic capital. This ratio can be calculated for each activity, department, unit, etc.

Figure 9. Estimation of the risk premium

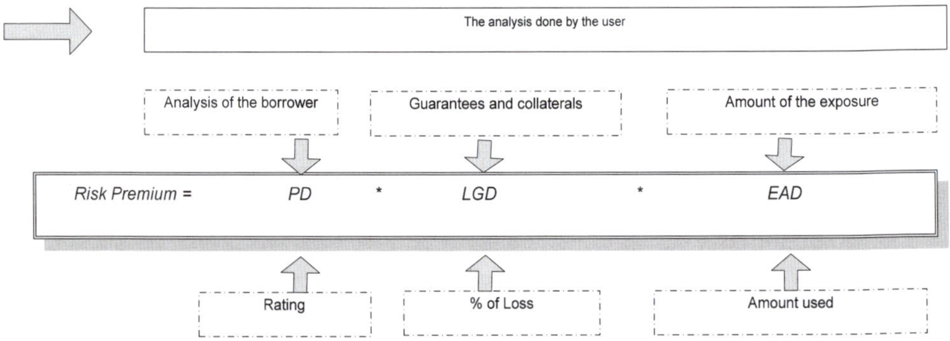

Source: Soley Sans & Rahnema (2004).

2.5 What is the likely impact of the CRD on SME financing in Europe?

In Europe, the majority of SMEs rely on loan financing as previously shown; however, another option exists for a bank – which is to finance companies through equity, either directly or through venture capital. Basel II and the CRD will impact SME financing, which may at a first sight raise some questions about the overall consequences of these changes. Although the new Basel capital rules will certainly impact the credit conditions for SMEs, they may not necessarily lead to a reduction of credit supply to these entities.

In terms of the cost of credit, Basel II will directly affect three components of the cost of credit to SMEs. First, the administrative or operational cost resulting from the processes to originate and manage loan portfolios may increase owing to the use of more sophisticated risk management tools that require greater investment in infrastructure (data collection, database maintenance and adequate modelling) and human resources. Second, there is *the cost of risk* composed of the cost of capital, which is the opportunity cost resulting from the fact that banks need regulatory and risk capital to cover loan exposures, and finally *the risk premium*, which is linked to the probability of default of the borrower, the exposure at default and the loss given default. The impact of the new banking regulatory rules on these latter two costs is not straightforward since it will depend on the risk characteristics of the borrowers (see Box 6).

Box 6. What impact does Basel II/CRD have on the cost of credit to SMEs?

The consumption of the credit institution's own resources (equity, subordinated debts and other reserves) has a direct relationship with the risk incurred by its credit and other operations. This is the essence of the risk premium, an important component of the cost of credit. Typically, the cost of credit includes:

- the refinancing cost, which is the price paid by the credit institution to its resource providers (the shareholders and other stakeholders);
- the administrative cost, which includes the cost of collecting, processing, analysing and evaluating the borrowers' information, the follow-up and the control of the different lines of credit;
- the cost of the credit institution's own resources (tier 1 and tier 2), which is the opportunity cost requested by the shareholders of the institution;
- the risk premium, which is the additional cost sought by the credit institution from each borrower to cover its expected and unexpected losses; and
- the credit institution margin, which is the profitability of the bank.

Basel II/CRD will have an effect on:

- the administrative cost, owing to the more sophisticated evaluation process of credit risk;
- the cost of the credit institution's own resources, because of its relationship to the consumption of capital, the risk of the portfolio and the higher capital requirements; and most importantly,
- the risk premium, by giving banks the opportunity to assess more effectively the risk incurred by its activities. This will be possible by introducing more risk-sensitive management techniques to assess distinct SME qualities. The risk premium will be lower when lending to good quality SMEs (or highly rated) and higher when lending to poor quality SMEs (or badly rated).

The more risk-sensitive pricing introduced by the new rules through the IRB approaches will entail a certain variation in capital adequacy, depending ultimately on the individual quality of the borrowers. A poor-quality borrower (rated B or CCC) will force its lender to hold more regulatory capital compared with a better-quality borrower (rated AAA or AA), but this does not ban loan financing.[77]

As shown in Figure 10, lending to small businesses under the IRB approach would reward highly rated businesses by only requiring banks to hold approximately 2% of capital charges as compared with 8% under the current Basel rules. The low-rated firms will cause their lenders to hold more than 8% of capital charges to tax the high risk inherent in this type of business. Under the standardised approach, the risk sensitivity of the new rules is lost, which means that a bank is required to hold the 8% of capital charges irregardless of the quality of the borrower.

Figure 10a. Capital charges by portfolio and approach: Medium to large corporations

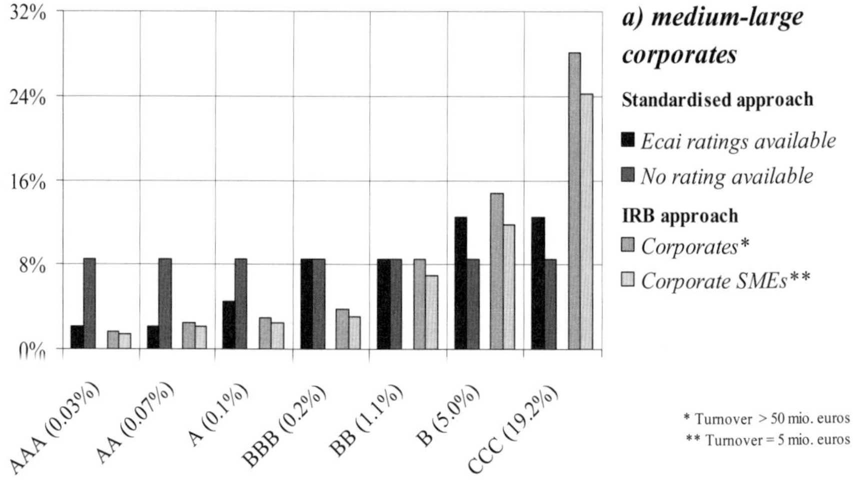

[77] Ayadi & Resti (2004).

Figure 10b. Capital charges by portfolio and approach: Small businesses and individuals*

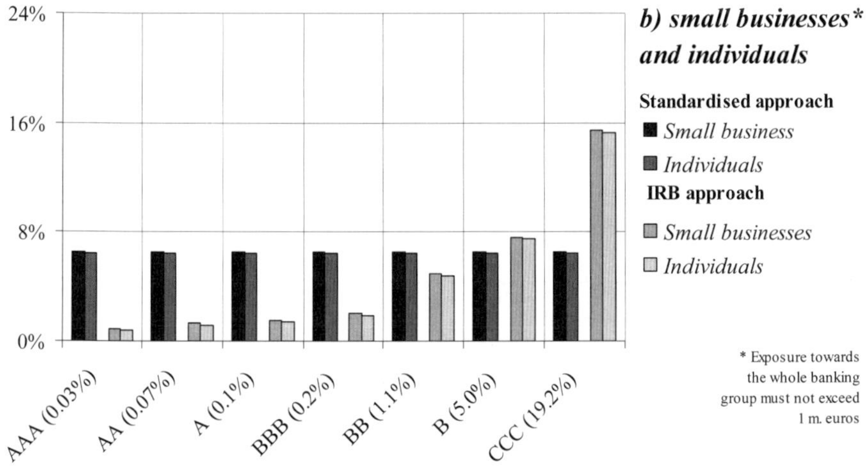

Source: Ayadi & Resti (2004).

On average, results from the third Quantitative Impact Study of European 'group 2' banks – those that are small and generally less complex and not internationally active – showed that no matter which category the SME exposure is assigned (to the corporate or the retail portfolio), the new regulatory capital rules will yield a lower SME risk weight compared with the existing framework (Table 17).

Moreover, as noted earlier, the European Commission report (2004a) on the consequences of the Basel II rules for all the sectors of the European economy with a particular focus on SMEs concludes that the new Accord should not have any negative impact on the availability and cost of finance for SMEs in most European countries. It points out that worries about an increase in the cost of finance owing to an increased use of internal ratings in lending activity are not justified. On the contrary, capital requirements relating to SME credit risks are expected to decrease, notably when using IRB approaches.

Other empirical studies[78] undertaken to assess the possible effects of Basel II implementation on SMEs in Europe generally find that the new

---

[78] See Schwaiger (2002) for the impact of Basel II on Austrian SMEs, Saurina & Trucharte (2004) for the impact on Spanish SMEs and Altman & Sabato (2005) for the impact on Italian SMEs.

banking rules lead to capital requirement savings linked to the SME segment when using one of the proposed approaches. When using the standardised approach, banks will enjoy more savings when SMEs are considered under the retail portfolio (the risk weight goes from 100 to 75%). When using one of the IRB approaches, banks are allowed to personalise the capital requirement calculations and build their own models to estimate PDs when using the foundation IRB approach and PDs, LGDs and other parameters when using the advanced IRB approach for each client.[79]

Table 17. Changes in the capital requirements (as compared with the present Accord) for 'group 2' banks: Total effect and contributions of individual sub-portfolios*

	Standardised (%)	Foundation IRB (%)
Sovereign	0.03	0.69
Bank	1.30	1.11
Retail (including small businesses)	-9.33	-22.46
Corporate	-0.74	-3.79
Corporate SMEs	-2.23	-4.93
Operational risk	9.41	6.36
Securitisation	0.07	-1.82
Trading portfolio	0.10	0.05
Specialised lending	-0.61	1.01
Equity	0.14	1.37
Receivables	0.00	0.00
Investments in related entities	0.64	1.12
Use of general provisions	0.00	-2.57
Total	-1.22	-23.86

**Small and generally less complex banks that are not internationally active.*

Source: European Commission (2003a). Individual data were weighted based on each bank's relevance inside its national system; national data were weighted according to the amount of regulatory capital (tier 1 + tier 2 - deductions) present under the current Accord in each of the 15 EU member states.

It should be borne in mind, however, that this average reduction does not mask a strong variation among banking institutions of different sizes

[79] See Heitfield (2004) who explains how banks should choose their own rating philosophy.

when adopting the standardised, foundation or advanced IRB approaches. Furthermore, different lending procedures and varying risk management expertise will lead to diverse outcomes throughout the banking industry, with better-rated banks able to manoeuvre more and lend at better rates. On the whole, it is very likely that banks opting for the more-advanced rating approaches would have a competitive advantage when lending to SMEs within the retail bracket.

Indeed, these different approaches will certainly generate differences in capital requirements for different quality SME portfolios, favouring to some extent the large internationally active banks that are more willing to adopt the advanced IRB approach and thus benefit from a considerable capital discount on highly rated SMEs, notably those treated as retail. The high risk-sensitivity of the IRB approaches would benefit the investment grade SMEs and penalise the riskier ones (say B-rated borrowers and below). The latter will be less expensive for banks adopting the standardised approaches; the opposite is true for highly rated SMEs.

The existence and the application of sophisticated credit-risk management tools will be a key element for banks to qualify for the advanced IRB approaches and in turn to ensure better risk-management of their credit portfolios, including the exposures to SMEs.

Small- or medium-sized banking institutions that have poorer internal risk-management systems and are unwilling to install more sophisticated tools will have to adopt the standardised approach, which is a fairly improved version of the current capital regulatory rules. This does not lead to capital charges for the SME portfolio that are different from the current rules (on average the 8% capital requirements are kept regardless of the rating of the borrower); but it would result in a deterioration of their asset quality since they do not have the adequate rating system to isolate and reject high-risk borrowers. The greater risk sensitivity introduced when using the foundation IRB implies low capital requirements in particular for good quality SMEs and relatively high capital requirements for poor quality ones (see Figure 11).

This is not necessarily bad news for SMEs, since a medium- to poor-quality borrower is better off asking for a loan from a bank using a standardised approach, whereas highly rated SMEs are better off asking for loans from IRB banks.

As previously explained, traditionally small and medium-sized banks are active locally and are the main supply sources of external finance to

SMEs. While they have a strong long-term relationship[80] with their clients based on local knowledge and experience (which helps to reduce information asymmetries), they may profit from their local dominant position by extracting 'rents' from SMEs, a situation that leads to higher charges. In this respect, it is important to monitor and ensure that anti-competitive behaviour is kept under the competition authorities' control.

Figure 11. Capital charges by approach and portfolio type: The standardised approach vs the IRB foundation approach

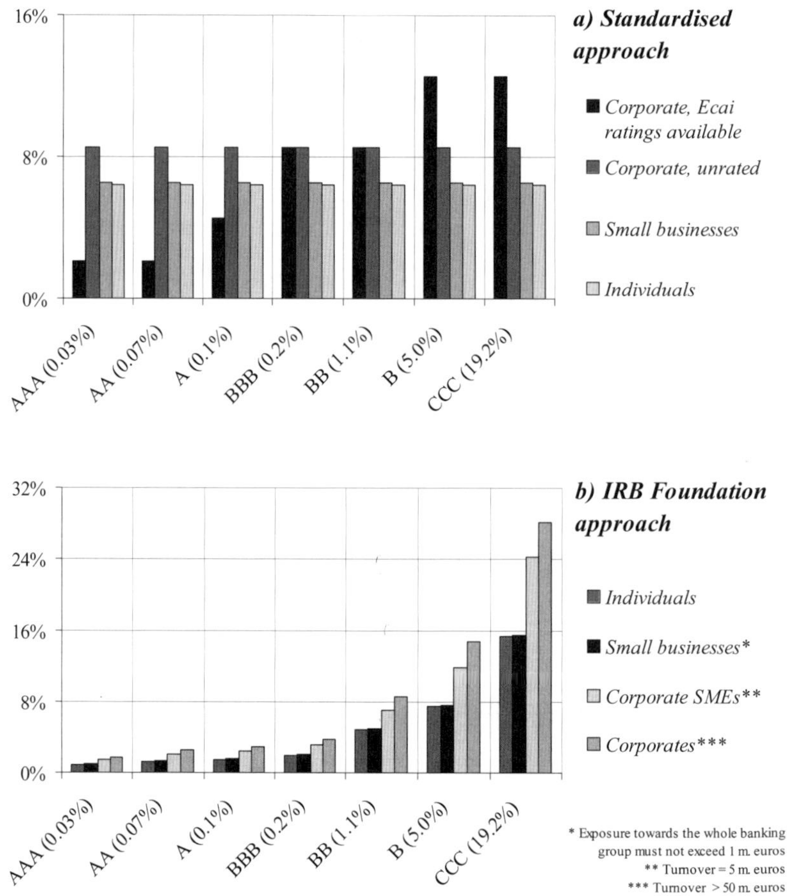

Source: Ayadi & Resti (2004).

---

[80] See Boot (2000).

Finally, the higher risk-sensitivity introduced in the new capital adequacy regime, while drawing a more precise picture of the creditworthiness of borrowers, is likely to raise capital charges in times of economic downturn. As a result, capital requirements may become a limitation for granting loans to SMEs and others, which in turn could intensify the economic slowdown. The pro-cyclical effect of the new Accord arises from the use of risk-sensitive techniques in the internal credit-risk systems. These effects are certainly different while using the standardised or the IRB approaches.

Indeed, according to a study by the Bank of England,[81] which sought to estimate the extent to which banks would downgrade loans in a recession, ratings based on Moody's approach lead to little, if any increase of capital requirements, whereas ratings based on a Merton-type model[82] lead to an increase of 40 to 50%.[83] The strong reactivity of the more sophisticated risk-assessment models (such as Merton-type models) is mainly related to the correlation of the probabilities of default to the economic cycle. Indeed, the probabilities of default are lower when the economic conditions are favourable and higher when the economy experiences a downturn. Confirming these conclusions, Altman et al. (2002) investigated the link between probabilities of default and loss given default and the effects of procyclicality on capital requirements. They found that banks that estimate probabilities of default and loss-given default had to reduce their credit portfolios to a larger extent, compared with banks that only estimate PDs and rely on supervisory estimates of LGDs. This finding provides clear evidence that the procyclicality of the Accord is more prominent when using the advanced IRB approach.

When the economy is in a downturn, the high risk-sensitivity of Basel II may indirectly exacerbate the deterioration of SME financial conditions since banks are more likely to cut credit because of the overall deterioration

---

[81] See Catarineu-Rabell et al. (2003).

[82] A Merton model or structural credit risk model was first proposed by Black and Scholes' and developed by Robert Merton in 1973 in his seminal paper on option pricing, as well as in a more detailed paper in 1974. Merton had in fact anticipated the model earlier in 1970. This fact, along with his active support of the work of Black and Scholes, is why the model is often referred to by his name.

[83] Similar results were found in Kashyap and Stein (2003); see also Jordan et al. (2003).

of the asset quality. At the same time, the payment behaviour of companies is very likely to deteriorate, which typically undermines SMEs' commercial transactions. This would create cash imbalances due to late payments, casting additional doubt on SMEs' creditworthiness and as a consequence would curb lending even more. Reduced lending would have a direct negative effect on growth, suggesting that some corrective measures should be put in place to avoid exacerbating the cycle.

Against this background, when asking bankers whether the new Basel Accord would make lending to SMEs less attractive in comparison with large companies, a survey by the European Investment Bank (Wagenvoort, 2003c) showed that roughly one out of four bankers still finds it difficult to assess the possible impact of Basel II on SME lending (see Figure 12).

Figure 12. The likely impact of Basel II on firm lending

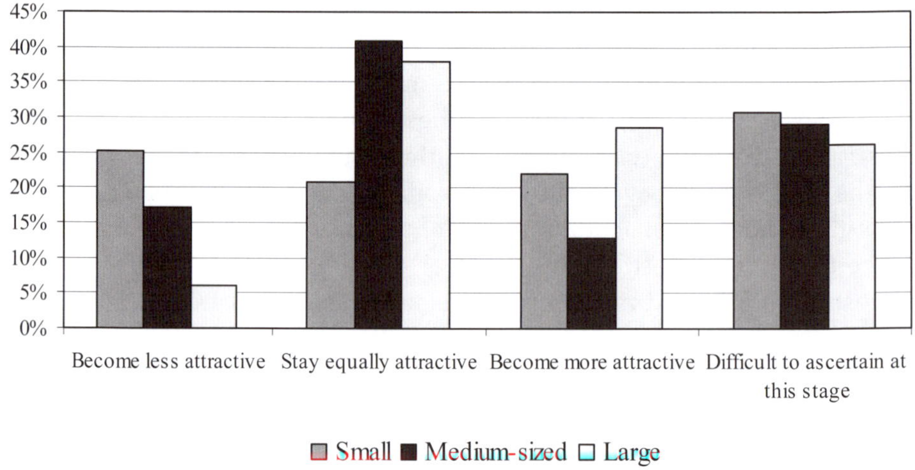

Source: Wagenvoort (2003c).

Around 40% of the bankers are of the opinion that lending to medium and large firms will remain equally attractive as under current banking regulation. With respect to small firms, only 20% of the respondents think that Basel II will be neutral for small-firm lending. Among those who expect Basel II to have an impact on loans to small firms, about half think that Basel II will stimulate lending while the other half anticipates a negative impact. In other words, it is expected that there will be banks reducing small-firm lending, but this reduction is likely to be offset by other banks that increase it. Recently, the McKinsey & Co. survey confirmed that an overwhelming majority of banks view the SME credit business as a core element of their portfolio and showed their interest in increasing it.

In terms of the practical implications for SME lending, the new IRB approaches to managing credit risk imply an increase of work to maintain updated and completed databases and to review the ratings and the factors involved in the modelling process more often. Indeed, there is a strong expectation that IRB banks will require their clients (notably SMEs under corporate and retail portfolios) to provide more, better structured, focused and timely data (financial statements, business plans, etc.) to complete their systems and to allow them to produce a precise and adequate ratings closely aligned to their risk profile over time. Covenants will become standard features of loan contracts (in particular ratings, leverage and liquidity) especially for long-term credit and the trend to collateralised lending as a means to mitigate credit risk will continue. The most tangible changes are the use of a more sophisticated statistical design to derive the ratings and the way this information is interpreted when using the most sophisticated statistical techniques to convert quantitative and qualitative data into ratings and probabilities of default, which will enhance the ability to identify potential future defaults. These changes will entail a much tighter and more systematic monitoring of creditworthiness of the borrower and credit risk overall. Yearly rating will be a common standard for banks to help identify problem loans. The monitoring process will be based on the data submitted yearly by the clients, and any delay in submission will serve as a warning signal and most likely lead to a downgrading. These conclusions were confirmed by the majority of banks in the McKinsey & Co. survey (European Commission, 2005b).

On the one hand, Basel II is a revolution in terms of improving risk management through the introduction of more risk-sensitive and more sophisticated tools borrowed from modern finance theories. But on the other hand, it may create a higher burden for some small enterprises (notably the potentially low-rated SMEs), which would need to provide well-structured and timely financial statements, to keep their bank accounts in a straight line with their agreements, to communicate any change (in the personnel and capital employed in the firm and arrange the successor matters), to provide adequate guarantees and collateral and to manage their credit function very carefully. These enterprises could still overcome the burden by internally managing their own risk: first, by investing in the accounting/financial function and ensuring they submit accurate and timely information about their financial situation to their banks; second, by implementing a viable credit management method that could be complemented by credit insurance to monitor their clients' payment behaviour and therefore to avoid bad payment habits or coverage in the event of insolvencies. This would in turn lead to a more stable cash flow and hence may improve the enterprise's creditworthiness.

Banks also have the alternative to finance SMEs in the first stages of their growth cycle through equity either directly or by investing in private equity or venture capital. Under the Basel I Accord, equity positions are risk-weighted at 100%, which does not correctly reflect their underlying risk profile. The risk weights assigned to these types of exposures, which are considered to be high-risk categories, are noticeably higher under the new Basel rules. The European Commission's CRD proposal has introduced lower-risk weights to such exposures, as compared with the original text of Basel II, but these are still considered to be higher than the current rules.

The new treatment may limit the attractiveness of this type of financing. The higher charges imposed on direct-equity financing and bank investments in private equity and venture capital business in Europe will inhibit banking institutions from investing in such businesses, as they are becoming very costly.[84]

Some SMEs, in particular those developing new technologies ('high-tech' SMEs) and relying to a certain extent on private equity and venture capital financing, will be somewhat affected by this treatment.[85] Indeed, developing new technologies is considered to be a risky business in addition to the uncertainty of expected returns, where the problem of information asymmetry is prominent.

---

[84] The role of banks in developing the European private equity and venture capital market is essential as banks contribute 25% of all capital committed (EVCA, 2004).

[85] According to a survey of European venture capital conducted by Bottazzi et al. (2004), almost 1,300 European firms were financed by European venture capitalists. These firms mainly belong to the high-technology industry.

3. Measures to improve SME financing under the new rating culture

Banks have been and will continue to be the most important source of financing for SMEs in Europe. Today, banks are facing a drastic change in the manner they usually conceive their business. Indeed, recent developments such as emerging risk-management techniques, financial innovation and other drivers linked to the high expectations of shareholders and regulators have brought new challenges for banks. Hence, they need to run their business with the most accurate tools not only to meet expectations but also to position themselves against fierce competition. In practice, banks must manage the risks to which they are exposed very carefully, with a specific focus on credit risk stemming from counterparties of varying risk quality. The SME sector is clearly one in which banks are looking to expand – first because SMEs have a high potential for innovation and flexibility and second because they foster growth. In parallel, the European Commission is committed to creating the best possible environment for SMEs to grow and to contribute to the realisation of the EU's Lisbon Agenda of March 2000.

The new requirements introduced by Basel II in parallel with the CRD mirror the trend in the financial industry towards more scientific risk-measurement and management. Since managing risks is the core of business of financial institutions, they ought to do it in the best possible way. Hence, the new regulation creates higher incentives for banks to assess the risk inherent in each individual exposure: riskier lending will be more expensive while safer lending will be less costly. In other words, for the banks that choose the IRB methods, there will be no room for cross-subsidisation. For these types of banks, credit decisions will be based on the individual risk quality of each borrower and his or her capacity to repay debt over time.

For SMEs, this will mean that their rating and probability of default are the determinant components for credit decisions (acceptance, rejection and conditions). They are also going to have a wider range of choices in terms of price and credit conditions. Since SMEs will not necessarily be aware of these changes, it is important that banks inform them. SMEs will also need to expend greater efforts and cooperate in a constructive way.

At the same time, the public sector should take action in terms of improving the general framework conditions of finance. Together with the markets, the public sector should act as a catalyst to encourage development.

3.1 The role of banks

As previously shown, gaps in information between borrowers and lenders are among the root causes of financing constraints for SMEs. The establishment of a long-term relationship based on increased transparency is key to reducing these information asymmetries.[86] The new banking regulations also cite increased transparency as a precondition for an effective cooperation between lenders and SMEs.

Banks should not hesitate to play their role by informing their customers about the changes and showing them how ratings impact their credit terms. Communication should not be limited to the reasons for not granting bank loans or withdrawing existing credit lines - it should be built upon mutual trust between banks and SMEs. Indeed, since ratings and associated probabilities of default are becoming the main factor for deciding whether or not a bank assigns or extends a line of credit, SMEs will need to be informed.

Therefore, bank procedures - including individual ratings, risk assessment and the factors leading to downgrading - will *need to be more transparent* to SMEs. In our interviews with banks, they were asked about their plans to disclose the rating process and individual ratings to their clients. Only a minority intend to disclose the individual ratings voluntarily. The majority plan to inform customers about the main drivers of the rating decision to enable them to address the necessary levers leading to an improved rating and to mitigate credit risk.[87] Obviously, a variety of views emanated from these interviews.

Against these different views, it is advisable to define minimum criteria on the level of the transparency required, which is not prejudicial to banks in terms of cost increases or competitiveness. Disclosing and explaining the overall detailed ratings process to potential clients could overburden a bank as it implies mobilising extra human resources. If the potential client becomes a loyal customer, the additional costs incurred by

---

[86] See Boot (2000).

[87] These conclusions were confirmed by the McKinsey & Co. survey (see European Commission 2005b).

the bank may be passed on as service costs to the customer. If the potential client is no longer interested or is shopping around to obtain the best ratings, then these costs will be a complete loss. Building on this point, it is crucial to define the right amount of disclosure that is both acceptable by banks and helpful to SMEs.

To explore this recommendation, our survey asked banks how they perceive an explicit regulation of ratings disclosure to loan applicants. The striking majority of respondents were not in favour of such a move since they think this would entail an extra regulatory burden.[88] In this respect, they consider that a non-legislative code of conduct between banks and SMEs should suffice to establish a framework that sets out principles on the disclosure of ratings and rating processes for banking and SME associations.

We strongly believe that a better disclosure of rating processes by banks will improve the new rating culture and also the SME–bank relationship in the rating process. It is therefore important to adequately define the principles that are the minimum requirements for governing this relationship. For example, before the rating process, banks need to inform SMEs about:

1) the data needed to determine the rating;
2) the factors affecting the credit decision (collateral, external ratings, etc.);
3) the principles of the rating system that will be applied (i.e. those covering the retail versus corporate categories); and
4) possible ways to improve the rating (better credit management, further guarantees, a more defined business plan, etc.).

After the rating process, banks need to communicate and explain the credit decision (acceptance, rejection or likely change of loan conditions) in a clear, comprehensible written manner. When updating the ratings (generally on an annual basis), banks need to inform their clients well in

---

[88] The adopted CRD stipulates that "banks are called upon to disclose their ratings decisions in writing and comprehensibly to SMEs and other corporate applicants for loans. Should a voluntarily undertaking by the sector in this regard prove inadequate, **national legislative measures** shall be adopted. The administrative costs for the banks have to be at an appropriate rate to the size of the loan" (emphasis added).

advance to provide the necessary inputs and again provide a written, comprehensible explanation of the changes.

3.2 The role of SMEs

Adopting one of the IRB approaches under the new banking regulation means that banks have to rely extensively on quantitative and qualitative information provided by SMEs. This information is essential for running the internal rating system properly. Companies that are well managed, adequately leveraged (equity ratio) and that provide timely, relevant and precise information will be in a position to obtain a better rating and consequently better credit conditions. Hence, it is crucial that companies understand and accommodate the new capital requirements in order to provide the most relevant data needed by lenders to rate their risk exposures. Below are the practical actions that SMEs must take to improve their ratings.[89]

General steps

1) Study and understand the bank requirements for granting a loan. Financial advice could be seen as an additional solution to make sure all the elements are taken into consideration.
2) Deliver clear, complete and timely financial and performance data needed by lenders to assign yearly ratings for granting a new loan or extending an existing line of credit with better conditions. Indeed, delayed submission of financial and performance data is seen to be a warning signal in many banks' internal rating systems. It usually leads to a downgrading and therefore price increases in new loan offers or the refusal of new loans.

Practical actions

3) Improve the factors that are considered to be important in the rating process, specifically:
   - Make sure that cash-flow stabilisation and generation receive priority among these efforts, since it is often the key tangible

---

[89] For more details, see the European Commission's (2005c) practical guide to loan financing for SMEs.

signal with which SMEs can negotiate their creditworthiness. This could be done by increasing and diversifying the sources of revenues (products and services), the customer and supplier's base and distribution channels, and implementing viable internal or external credit-management procedures to monitor clients' payment behaviour (receivables) and therefore avoid bad payment habits. Late payment habits from clients should be limited since the late or irregular cashing-in of revenues could easily drag down the rating and, by limiting the perceived debt capacity of the firm, may adversely affect company growth. In addition to legislative efforts to combat such malpractices (e.g. the EU's late payment directive), many companies could directly take action by (for example) using credit insurance policies to prevent and minimise late payments and defaults. Credit insurance could offer a complete risk-management tool that helps management to put in place the necessary procedures to continuously monitor the creditworthiness of clients and reduce the risk of delays and defaults.

- Increase the equity base by preferring retained earnings over distributed profits.
- Improve the accounting, controlling and management methods within the company where these need attention. Entrepreneurs should not only give more importance to the accounting and financial functions within the company but also move towards more active balance-sheet (or asset liability) management in terms of reducing the mismatch between long-term commitment versus cash. SMEs should also consider how they manage their liabilities as a means to increase competitiveness. In this respect, innovation could serve them very well – as it has served banks – to reduce the overall amount of risk through the active management of liabilities.
- Consolidate the business development strategy, encourage strategic thinking among managers in terms of the business prospects, undertake market/sector/activity analyses and improve external communications with stakeholders.
- Renew the attention given to some aspects of the business that may have been neglected, such as keeping bank accounts in line with agreements, communicating any changes in the personnel or

capital employed in the firm, and determining successor arrangements for key staff.

- Put in place recovery procedures in the event of crisis scenarios such as the loss of a key person in the company, the revaluation of a national currency for companies that heavily rely on exports, etc.

4) Ensure that adequate guarantees and collateral are provided. Collateral and guarantees help to obtain better loan conditions. As previously noted, the loan pricing policy is mainly influenced by rating, term structure (maturity) and collateral. SMEs need to be able to provide adequate collateral. The list of credit-risk mitigation techniques in Basel II and the CRD is extensive, but these ultimately depend on the expected recovery rate (which is a related variable of the LGD). For example, the expected recovery rate of cash is almost 100%, while the expected recovery rate for receivables is between 60 and 95%. It is advisable for SMEs to look at other types of collateral such as credit insurance, which again could offer an indemnification for accounts receivable to increase their value when recovery is required in the case of default. Credit insurance could also serve as a protection for SMEs in countries with high political risks.

Other specific actions

5) Work more proactively to increase equity finance. Many SMEs need stronger balance sheets. Venture capital, equity finance and business angels are more readily accessible to SMEs that can show high growth potential.

6) Consider different financing sources. Although it is true that the main financing products are provided by banks, it is important for SMEs to be able to compare different financing sources to judge which is more appropriate to the risk level of the company according to its growth cycle. Leasing, factoring and other sources could offer a good response to SMEs willing to investigate other financing means, particularly for those that have more difficulties providing well-structured financial and performance data – the basic prerequisites to accessing finance through banks.

3.3 The role of public policy

Improving access to finance is an important aspect of fostering entrepreneurship and growth in Europe. Many actions have been already been taken at the European and national levels to improve access to finance. The purpose of this section is not to enumerate these actions but to suggest some improvements to enhance the environment for SME financing in the post-Basel II/CRD era.

1) There is room for continued improvement in the relationship between banks and SMEs in the new rating culture. Thus it is important to establish a non-legislative framework (code of conduct) that sets out the principles for defining minimum criteria for ratings disclosure.

2) Access to equity finance could also be improved. As equity finance is included in the high-risk category under Basel II and the CRD, banks are likely to withdraw from these investments owing to the high risk weights assigned to them. At the same time, many SMEs need stronger balance sheets that can be translated into a higher equity ratio. Hence, at the regional, national and European levels, it is important to focus on developing European venture capital markets and their liquidity, and to promote the possibilities provided by business angels and their networks.

3) Since a stronger equity base is a reflection of higher creditworthiness, it is important to recognise that retained earnings are the best form of financing growth and investment. National governments should review whether their tax laws obstruct firm growth by taxing retained earnings more than distributed profits.

4) Legislative efforts to combat late payment habits need to continue and be reinforced to ensure better stabilisation of cash flows, which are a prerequisite for better ratings.

BIBLIOGRAPHY

Ade, B., T. Heimer, F. Loch, T. Lehmann and V. Steimle (2003), *The New Framework for Capital Adequacy (Basel II), Consequences for Small and Medium-sized Enterprises (SMEs) and Presentation of Political Options for the Implementation*, Background paper prepared for the European Parliament, EB/IV/A/2003/07/02, Hochschule fur Bankwirtschaft (HfB), Frankfurt.

Altman, E.I. and G. Sabato (2005), *Global effects of the new Basel Capital Accord's implementation on SMEs,* Discussion paper presented at the conference of the Swedish Network for European Studies in Economics and Business in Molle, May.

Altman, E., A. Resti and A. Sironi (2002), *The Link between Default and Recovery Rates, Effects of the Procyclicality on Capital Requirements*, BIS Working Paper No. 113, Bank for International Settlements, Basel.

Ayadi, R. and F. De Rossi (2004a), *Practical implications of the new Basel Capital Accord for the European financial system: Results and analysis of an industry survey*, Centre for European Policy Studies, Brussels (see http://www.ceps.be/Article.php?article_id=349).

-------- (2004b), *Facing the Credit Squeeze: Effects of the Capital Adequacy and Late Payments Directives on SMEs*, Report of a joint CEPS-Intrum Justitia roundtable, Centre for European Policy Studies, Brussels, November (see http://shop.ceps.be).

Ayadi, R. and A. Resti (2004), *The New Basel Capital Accord and the Future of the European Financial System*, CEPS Task Force Report No. 51, Centre for European Policy Studies, Brussels, April.

Bank of International Settlements (BIS) (1988), *International convergence of capital measurements and capital standards*, July, Basel.

-------- (2000), *Range of practice in banks' internal ratings systems*, BIS, Basel, January.

-------- (2001a), *Consultative Document – The New Basel Capital Accord*, BIS, Basel, January.

-------- (2001b), "Progress towards the completion of the new Basel Capital Accord", Press release, BIS, Basel, December.

-------- (2002), "Basel Committee reaches agreements on new Capital Accord issues", Press release, BIS, Basel, July.

-------- (2003a), *Consultative Document – The New Basel Capital Accord*, BIS, Basel, April.

-------- (2003b), *Quantitative Impact Study 3 – Overview of Global Results*, BIS, Basel, May.

-------- (2003c), *Supplementary Information on QIS-3, Bank for International Settlements*, BIS, Basel, May.

-------- (2003d), "Basel II: Significant progress on major issues", Press release, BIS, Basel, October.

-------- (2004), *International convergence of capital measurements and capital standards – A revised framework*, BIS, Basel, June.

Berger, A.N. (2004), *Potential competitive effects of Basel II on banks in SME credit markets in the United States*, Board of Governors of the Federal Reserve System, Washington, D.C. February.

Berger, A.N. and G.F. Udell, (1998), "The economics of small business finance: The roles of private equity and debt markets in the financial growth cycle", *Journal of Banking and Finance*, Vol. 22, pp. 613-73.

Berger, A.N., A. Saunders, J.M. Scalise and G.F. Udell (1998), "The effects of bank mergers and acquisitions on small business lending", *Journal of Financial Economics*, Vol. 50, pp. 187-229.

Boot, A.W.A. (2000), "Relationship banking: What do we know?", *Journal of Financial Intermediation*, Vol. 9, pp. 7–25.

Bottazzi, L., M. Da Rin and T. Hellmann (2004), "The changing face of the European venture capital industry: Facts and analysis", *Journal of Private Equity*, Vol. 8, No. 1, Winter.

Catarineu-Rabell, E., P. Jackson and D. Tsomocos (2003), *Procyclicality and the New Basel Accord, Banks' Choice of Loan Granting System*, Working Paper No. 181, Bank of England, London.

Creditreform (2003), *Insolvenzen in Europa, Jahr 2002/2003*, Neuss.

Crouhy, M., D. Galai and R. Mark (2001), "A comparative analysis of current credit risk models", *Journal of Banking and Finance*, Vol. 24, pp. 59-117.

Euler Hermes (2005), *The role and the importance of credit insurance in credit management*, A survey of UK businesses by the Credit Management Research Centre for Euler Hermes, London, April.

European Commission (2000), *The European Observatory for European SMEs, Sixth Report*, The European Observatory for SMEs, prepared by KPMG and EIM Small Business Research Consultancy, in cooperation with the European Network for SME Research, Luxembourg.

-------- (2001), *Enterprises' access to finance*, Commission Staff Working Paper, SEC (2001) 1667, Brussels, October.

-------- (2002), *SMEs in Europe, including a first glance at EU candidate countries*, The European Observatory for SMEs, Report No. 2, Luxembourg: Enterprise Publications.

-------- (2003), *The European Observatory for European SMEs, SMEs and access to finance*, Brussels.

-------- (2003a), *Review of the Capital Requirements for Credit Institutions and Investment Firms – Third Quantitative Impact Study: EU Results*, Brussels, July.

-------- (2003b), "Review of the Capital Requirements for Credit Institutions and Investment Firms, Third Quantitative Impact Study: Methodological Annex", mimeo, Brussels, July.

-------- (2003c), *Commission recommendations of 06/05/2003 concerning the definition of micro, small and medium-sized enterprises*, Brussels.

-------- (2003d), *Review of Capital Requirements for Banks and Investment Firms*, Commission Services Third Consultation Paper, Brussels, July.

-------- (2003e), *Review of the Capital Requirements for Credit Institutions and Investment Firms*, Brussels (retrievable at: www.bis.org/bcbs/qis/QIS-3).

-------- (2003f), Access to finance of small and medium-sized enterprises, Communication from the Commission to the Council and the European Parliament, December, Brussels.

-------- (2004a), *Study on the financial and macroeconomic consequences of the draft proposed new capital requirements for banks and investment firms*, Study prepared by PricewaterhouseCoopers and the National Institute for Economic and Social Research, MARKT/2003/02/F, Brussels.

-------- (2004b), *The new capital requirements for banks and investments firms*, July, Brussels.

-------- (2004c), *Code of conduct between credit institutions and SMEs*, Commission Staff Working Document, Brussels.

-------- (2005), *Credit insurance for European SMEs – A guide to assessing the need to manage liquidity risk*, Brussels.

-------- (2005a), *The new SME definition: User's guide and model declaration*, Brussels.

-------- (2005b), *Results from the survey of European banks*, Survey undertaken by McKinsey and Company and Company and System Consulting Network S.r.l (Notably Prof. Riccardo De Lisa) , May, Brussels.

-------- (2005c), *How to deal with the new rating culture – A practical guide to loan financing for small and medium-sized enterprises*, Study undertaken by McKinsey and Company and System Consulting Network S.r.l (Notably Prof. Riccardo De Lisa), July, Brussels.

European Network for SME Research (2002), Enterprise Survey (retrieved from http://europa.eu.int/comm/enterprise/enterprise_policy/analysis/observatory_en.htm).

European Network for SME Research (2003), Enterprise Survey (retrieved from http://europa.eu.int/comm/enterprise/enterprise_policy/analysis/observatory_en.htm).

European Private Equity and Venture Capital Association (EVCA) (2004), *Further comments to the Basel committee: The risk profile of private equity and venture capital*, February.

Exco, Grant & Thornton Survey (2001), *Enterprises' access to finance*, Annual survey on SMEs, published as European Commission (2001), Commission Staff Working Paper, SEC (2001) 1667, Brussels, October.

Global Conference on Credit Scoring (2001), *Conference Proceedings*, 2-3 April, Washington, D.C.

Greater London Enterprise Ltd. (2003), *Analysis of Use of Factoring*, London.

Heitfield, E. (2004), *Rating system dynamics and bank-reported default probabilities under the new Basel Capital Accord*, Federal Reserve Board, Washington, D.C. (retrieved from www.defaultrisk.com).

Intrum Justitia (2005), *European Payment Index: All time high number of insolvencies – Lower payment risks*, Stockholm, Spring.

Jordan, J., J. Peek and E. Rosengren (2003), *Credit risk modelling and the cyclicality of capital*, Working Paper, Federal Reserve Bank of Boston.

Kashyap, A.K. and J.C. Stein (2003), *Cyclical implications of the Basel II capital standards*, Working Paper, University of Chicago, Chicago, Il.

Leaseurope (2002), *Leasing activity in Europe: Key facts and figures,* Brussels.

Mercer Oliver Wyman (2004), *The Future of Business Banking in Europe,* NY, January (retrieved from http://www.merceroliverwyman.com).

Ong, M.K. (2003), *Internal credit risk models: Capital allocation and performance measurements,* London: Risk Books.

-------- (2004), *The Basel Handbook: A guide for financial practitioners,* London: Risk Books.

Prowse, S. (1998), "Angel investors and the market for angel investments", *Journal of Banking and Finance,* Vol. 22, pp. 785-92.

Sahlman, W.A. (1990), "The structure and governance of venture capital organisations", *Journal of Financial Economics,* pp. 471-521.

San José Riestra, A. (2002), *Credit Bureaus in Today's Credit Markets,* ECRI Research Report No. 4, Centre for European Policy Studies, Brussels, September.

-------- (2003), *Credit Insurance in Europe: Impact, Measurement and Policy Recommendations,* CEPS Research Report in Banking and Finance, No. 31, Centre for European Policy Studies, Brussels, February.

Saurina, J. and C. Trucharte (2004), "The impact of Basel II on lending to small- and medium-sized firms: A regulatory policy assessment based on Spanish credit register data", *Journal of Finance Services Research,* Vol. 26, pp. 121-44.

Schure, P., R. Wagenvoort, and D. O'Brien (2004), "The efficiency and conduct of European banks, developments after 1992", *Review of Financial Economics,* Vol. 13.

Schwaiger, W.S.A. (2002), *Basel II: Quantitative Impact Study on Austrian Small and Medium-sized Enterprises,* Technical University of Vienna.

Soley Sans, J. and A. Rahnema (2004), *Basilea II: Una nueva forma de relacion Banca-Empresa,* IESE Business School, New York: McGraw Hill.

Standard & Poor's (S&P) (2003), see http://www.standardsandpoors.com.

Stiglitz, J.E. and A. Weiss (1981) "Credit rationing in markets with imperfect information", *American Economic Review,* No. 71/3, pp. 393-410.

Udell, G.F. (2004), *SME lending: Defining the issues in a global perspective,* Working Paper, Kelley School of Business, Indiana University.

Wagenvoort, R. (2003a), "Are finance constraints hindering the growth of SMEs on Europe?", *EIB Papers*, Vol. 2, No. 2, European Investment Bank, Luxembourg.

-------- (2003b), "SME finance in Europe, introduction and overview", *EIB Papers*, Vol. 2, No. 2, European Investment Bank, Luxembourg.

-------- (2003c), *Bank survey evidence on bank lending to SMEs in the European Union*, Economic and Financial Report 2003/01, European Investment Bank, Luxembourg.

Wetzel Jr., W.E (1994), "Venture Capital" in W.D. Bygrave (ed.), *The Portable MBA in Entrepreneurship*, New York: John Wiley & Sons, pp. 172-94.

World Bank (2004), *Financing small and medium-sized enterprises with factoring: Global growth in factoring and its potential in Eastern Europe*, a joint publication of the World Bank's private and financial sector development department and the development economics research group, Washington, D.C., May.

ANNEXES

ANNEX 1. WHAT IS THE CREDIT RISK PREMIUM?

By taking credit risk and the length of the lending period into account, differences in nominal interest rates, at a point in time, can be explained with the following equation:

$$i_{market} = \{r^* + E(\pi_t)\} + \rho + \lambda$$

The first two components in brackets are the desired rate of return and the expected inflation that make up the core of any interest rate at a point in time. The third component 'ρ' is known as the 'risk premium' established by credit markets for different categories of risk. This value depends on how risk-averse lenders might be at any point of time. The last component 'λ' is known as the liquidity premium, which represents the amount of compensation required by the lender for lending to the long end of the market. Let us take an example based on different nominal interest rates and different levels of risk associated with a certain class of borrowers, as shown in Table A.1.

Table A.1. Nominal interest rates and different levels of risk for a certain class of borrowers

	No risk	**Low risk**	**Medium risk**	**High risk**
Term	Treasury	AAA-AA	A-BB	B-CC
Short-term (1 year or less)	1.80%	3.36%	3.95%	5%
Medium-term (1-10 years)	4.24%	4.46%	5.12%	8%
Long-term (+10 years)	5.54%	6.21%	6.89%	10%

Source: Based on Standard & Poor's (2003).

Each column represents a different level of risk associated with a particular category of borrowers. This risk is also known as the credit risk, whereby different types of borrowers (or related projects) have different probabilities of being able to make scheduled interest payments and to repay the principle of the debt. These risk categories are commonly established by various credit agencies, the most popular being Standard & Poor's (S&P) and Moody's.

The no-risk category corresponds to the government debt (T-bills, T-notes and T-bonds). In this category, there is an absolute certainty that the borrower will be able to properly make scheduled interest payments and repay the principle of the debt. The low-risk category corresponds to S&P's classification of AAA-AA, called 'investment grade lending'. Borrowers in this category have a strong history of debt repayment and a strong steam of revenues to service any future debt. Lending under this category is considered to be for the very risk-averse, who seek to protect their asset base by avoiding the borrowers who might default in their debt repayment.

The classification A-BB represents the somewhat speculative grade of medium-risk lending. Borrowers in this category often have a good credit history; however, some uncertainty about future revenues to service additional debt persists. Lenders involved in these types of loans are willing to speculate that all interest payments and principal repayments will take place in return for a slightly higher return on their investment.

Finally, the high-risk category carries a B-CCC rating, also known as 'junk' or highly speculative lending. Lenders in this category are willing to put their assets at risk in return for a high return, given the strong probability of default carried by this type of asset. Given these risk categories, the risk premium is the reward or the additional return for holding a risky investment rather than a risk-free one.

ANNEX 2. SME CAPITAL REQUIREMENT FORMULAS

For the SMEs classified as retail, the capital requirement formulas correspond to the formulas given for other retail exposures. For SMEs in the corporate portfolio, the formulas used are those for the corporate category, considering the size discount.

Table A.2. Formulas used for SMEs in the retail and corporate portfolios

SMEs in the retail portfolio	SMEs in the corporate portfolio
Correlation = R = 0,03*(1-EXP(-35*PD))/(1-EXP(-35)) + 0,16*[1-(1-EXP(-35*PD))/1-EXP(-35)]	Correlation = R = 0,12*(1-EXP(-50*PD))/(1-EXP(-50)) + 0,24*[1-(1-EXP(-50*PD))/1-EXP(-50)] – 0,04*(1-(S-5)/45)
Capital requirements = K= LGD*N((1-R)^(-0,5)*G(PD)+(R/(1-R)^0,5)*G(0,999))-PD*LGD	Capital requirements = K= LGD*N((1-R)^(-0,5)*G(PD)+(R/(1-R)^0,5)*G(0,999))-PD*LGD*(1-1,5*b)^(-1*(1+(M-2,5)*b))
G(x) is the inverse of the standard normal cumulative distribution function	Maturity adjustment = b= (0,11852-0,05478*LN(PD)^2)

Source: BIS (2004).

Annex 3. A Glance at the Treatment of Purchased Receivables under Basel II*

Eligible purchased receivables are divided into retail and corporate receivables. SME receivables fall under both categories.

1. If SME receivables are qualified under the *retail category,* the purchasing bank that complies with the internal ratings-based (IRB) rules for retail exposures is eligible for the following 'top-down' approach. For this type of asset, there are IRB charges for both default risk and dilution risk.

   To assess the default risk, the bank must provide estimates for probability of default (PD) and loss-given default (LGD) for the receivables on a stand-alone basis without regard to any assumption of recourse or guarantees from the seller or other parties.

   Dilution refers to the possibility that the receivable amount is reduced through cash or non-cash credit to the receivables' obligor. Examples include offsets or allowances arising from returns of goods sold, disputes regarding product quality, possible debts of the borrower to a receivable obligor and any payment or promotional discount offered by the borrower (e.g. a credit for cash payments within 30 days). To assess dilution risk, the purchasing bank must estimate a one-year expected loss for dilution risk also expressed in a percentage of the receivables amount. To estimate the expected loss, the bank can utilise external and internal data and the estimate must be computed on a stand-alone basis. To calculate the risk weights for dilution risk, the PD must be set equal to the estimated expected loss and the LGD must be set at 100%; a one-year maturity could be applied under the supervisory discretion. This treatment applies to whether underlying receivables are corporate or retail exposures.

2. If SME receivables are qualified under the corporate category, their treatment depends on whether they are eligible for the top-down

* *Source:* BIS (2004).

approach or not. To be eligible for treatment under this approach, they must satisfy the following conditions:

a) They must be purchased from unrelated, third-party sellers.

b) They must be generated on an arm's length basis between the seller and the obligor.

c) The purchasing bank has a claim on the proceeds from the pool of receivables or a pro-rata interest in the proceeds (first loss position, second loss position, etc.).

d) The supervisor must set a concentration limit above which capital requirements should be calculated. The concentration limit may refer to the following parameters: the size of one individual exposure relative to the total pool, the size of the pool of receivables as a percentage of regulatory capital or the maximum size of an individual exposure in the pool.

To assess the default risk in the eligible purchased corporate receivables, two approaches apply.

a) Under the IRB foundation approach, if the purchasing bank is unable to decompose the expected loss into its PD and LGD in a reliable manner, the risk weight is determined from the corporate risk weight function using the following specifications:

   - If the bank can demonstrate that the exposures are exclusively senior claims to corporate borrowers, an LGD of 45% is used; PD is then calculated by dividing the expected loss by this given LGD.
   - If the PD is a bank's estimate of the expected loss, LGD is set to be 100%.

   If the purchasing bank is able to estimate PD in a reliable manner, the risk weight is determined from the corporate risk weight functions according to the specifications of LGD, maturity (m) and the treatment of guarantees under the foundation approach.

b) Under the advanced IRB approach, the purchasing bank will provide estimates of the risk parameters internally.

   If the purchased corporate receivables are not eligible for this treatment, their default risk will be assessed as other corporate exposures.

ANNEX 4. CEPS' SURVEY ON THE POTENTIAL EFFECTS OF THE BASEL II FRAMEWORK ON SME FINANCING*

HOW TO FILL IN THE QUESTIONNAIRE

1) Answer if your institution is a **bank** or another **financial enterprise** liable to the application of the new prudential regulation (CAD III-Basel II). If you are a representative of a **banking association**, please forward this questionnaire to your members.
2) In case of **multiple choices** please use **numbers** to **rank** your answers (start from 1 = the most important and **avoid any duplication**).
3) Please note that data will be treated in aggregate for the only purpose of internal statistical analysis. CEPS ensures **full confidentiality** on responses.

GENERAL INFORMATION

Name:.. Tel:...

Division/Position:............................. Email:.......................................

Company:....................................... Country:...................................

Sector of activity:...

Purpose of the questionnaire

The creation of the best possible environment for entrepreneurship is at the heart of the strategy launched by the European Council in Lisbon. Nevertheless, the forthcoming new CRD has sparked concerns that higher capital charges will further curb lending to SMEs. Actually, the new banking regulation intends to enhance the efficiency of credit allocation by giving incentives to a more risk sensitive pricing introduced by the internal ratings-based approaches. This will certainly entail variance in capital adequacy depending on the individual quality of the SME. As a

* The author would like to acknowledge the research assistance of Francesco De Rossi in the preparation of this survey.

consequence, the availability of loan financing will be more conditional on an enterprise's financial strength and its ability to provide relevant quantitative and qualitative information. A particular prerequisite to improve the enterprise's financial strength is a smoother settlement of commercial transactions.

The CEPS survey aims at providing statistical evidence to help understand banks' rating procedures, SMEs' financial structure, and the effects of late payments in an atmosphere of dynamic repositioning due to the forthcoming banking regulation. The results will serve to publish a CEPS report on *The New Basel Capital Accord and SME Financing: SMEs and the New Rating Culture,* expected to be released in mid-2005.

This questionnaire should be directed to the audit, compliance or risk department of your bank.

Banks and Other Financial Institutions

1. What is the asset size of your financial institution?

☐ less than €100 million in assets ☐ between €100 and €500 million

☐ between €500 million and €1 billion ☐ between €1 and €10 billion

☐ more than €10 billion in assets

2. How does your institution intend to comply with the new regulation as regards the computation of capital requirements against credit risk?

☐ Standardised Approach (SA)

☐ Internal Rating Based (IRB) Approach in the foundation version

☐ Advanced IRB approach

☐ Partial adoption of the IRB approach (with the use of the Standardised Approach for financial institutions' and sovereigns' exposures).

3. What is the importance of SME financing for the business of your institution?

☐ marginal (less than 5% of the assets)

☐ relevant (between 5% and 20% of the assets)

☐ very important (between 20% and 40% of the assets)

☐ predominant (more than 40% of the assets)

Comments……………………………………………………………………………

4. What proportion of your institution's overall SME exposure fulfils the requirements (small and granular credits) to be qualified as retail portfolio?

☐ less than 20% ☐ between 20% and 50%

☐ between 50% and 70% ☐ more than 70%

5. Please provide a brief description of the composition of your institution's SME portfolio in terms of credit quality.

☐ ....% of SME exposures has very little risk (top rating)

☐ ....% of SME exposures has a moderate risk (good rating)

☐ ....% of SME exposures is reasonably risky (decent rating)

☐ ....% of SME exposures is risky (low rating)

☐ ....% of SME exposures has a high risk (bad rating)

☐ ....% of SME exposures has already shown difficulties (past due loans, etc.)

Others/comments...

6. What types of techniques are generally used by your institution to decide whether to provide credit or not, and under what conditions, to SMEs?

- ☐ financial statement analysis with a strong focus at the applicant firm level
- ☐ the applicant firm is sorted into credit merit clusters by means of quantitative methods based on 'hard' information (market analysis, macroeconomic indicators, balance sheets ratios, cash flow and financial statement data)
- ☐ use of 'soft' information directly collected by loan officials from past or similar credit relationships (such as knowledge of local businesses, or of personal, credit and entrepreneurial past history of managers and owners of the firm)
- ☐ credit granting considerably relies upon the external ratings of the applicant firm
- ☐ credit scoring, the applicant is assigned a 'score' by quantitative methods that elaborate on 'hard' information and, at least for the part that can be captured by index variables, on 'soft' information also
- ☐ requests of funding are mostly assessed on grounds of collateral presented
- ☐ a mix of these techniques or others, please give some comments:.................

If your institution provides internal ratings to SME exposures, please spend an extra moment to clarify some technical details about:

a) What are the elements you include in loan pricing?

....

b) What is the rating scale adopted?

....

c) How does your institution translate 'credit scores' into ratings?

....

d) What is the link between the rating scale and the estimates of the probability of default (PD) and loss given default (LGD) required by Basel II adopted by your institution?

....

7. To the extent that your institution assesses applicants' creditworthiness by processing 'hard' information (financial statements, credit scoring and other quantitative methods), the relevant datasets are obtained from:

   □ your own bank databases

   □ private external credit bureaus

   □ public credit registries

   □ membership in cooperative credit bureaus

8. How often does your bank update its internal credit risk assessment (ratings)?

   □ each quarter or more often   □ twice a year

   □ about once per year   □ once every two years or more

9. Please indicate which, if any, of the following events generally cause downgrading of SMEs according to the assessment of your institution:

   Macroeconomic factors

   □ worsening of macroeconomic conditions

   □ increase of sovereign risk of the country where SMEs are located

   □ tightening of monetary conditions (high interest rates)

   □ higher volatility of commodity prices

   □ reduction of exports

   □ exchange rate appreciation

   Others...

   Business and financial factors

   □ loss of market shares

   □ expansion in new and unexplored businesses

   □ lower innovation capacity (for instance measured through R&D investments)

   □ increase in long-term debt

   □ liquidation of financial assets

   □ increase in outstanding trade credit

   □ increase in merchandise disputes with suppliers/clients

   □ late payments from clients

   Others...

   Factors related to governance

   □ separation of ownership from control

   □ change of managers

   □ drop of relationship with the firm's principal creditor (generally a bank)

   □ loss of technical personnel

   □ change/death of principal owner/s

   Others...

10. Please identify the risk mitigation techniques generally used by your company to secure exposures to SMEs.

☐ mortgages of commercial real estate specifically to secure long-term credit

☐ pledge of inventories and equipment to secure short/medium-term loans

☐ to secure short/medium-term loans financial assets are generally preferred

☐ pledge of financial assets is required also to secure long-term loans

☐ personal guarantees from the principal owner/s†

☐ guarantees from affiliate or parent firms

☐ credit derivatives/insurance

Others……………………………………………………………………………………

Please indicate the major effects of the provision of guarantees from SMEs:

☐ crucial to grant credit

☐ lowers the cost of credit

☐ increases credit lines and/or extends their duration

☐ consents to relax or avoid some tight credit covenants

☐ a mix of these effects, please explain…………………………………………………

Others……………………………………………………………………………………

11. Does your institution provide factoring facilities to SMEs?

☐ no

☐ accounts receivable are discounted but not within proper factoring agreements

☐ yes, but mainly agency factoring (sales ledger and debt collection)

☐ yes, about ……% of our SME financing derives from factoring invoices, and ……% of these contracts are signed under non-recourse terms

---

† Such as mortgages on residential properties or other pledges of personal estate. Please remember to include, if any, similar pledges from the principal owner's direct associates.

Recent CEPS Publications*

CEPS Paperbacks

Europe's Hidden Capital Markets: Evolution, Architecture and Regulation of the European Bond Market, Jean-Pierre Casey and Karel Lannoo, November 2005

Democratisation in the European Neighbourhood, Michael Emerson (ed.), October 2005

Readings in European Security, Vol. 3, Dana H. Allin and Michael Emerson (eds), October 2005

Migration, Borders & Asylum: Trends and Vulnerabilities in EU Policy, Thierry Balzacq and Sergio Carrera, July 2005

Deep Integration: How Transatlantic Markets are Leading Globalization; Daniel S. Hamilton and Joseph P. Quinlan (eds), published jointly with the Center for Transatlantic Relations of Johns Hopkins University, June 2005

EMU at Risk, Daniel Gros, Thomas Mayer and Angel Ubide, 7th Annual Report of the CEPS Macroeconomic Policy Group, June 2005

CEPS Task Force Reports

No. 58 *Achieving a Common Cnosolidated Corporate Tax Base in the EU*, Malcolm Gammie, Silvia Giannini, Alexander Klemm, Andreas Oestreicher, Paola Parascandolo and Christoph Spengel, November 2005

No. 57 *Reviewing the EU Emissions Trading Scheme: Priorities for Short-Term Implementation of the Second Round of Allocation*, Christian Egenhofer and Noriko Fujiwara, August 2005

No. 56 *Market Stimulation of Renewable Electricity in the EU: What Degree of Harmonisation to Support Mechanisms is Required?*, Jaap Jansen, Kyriakos Gialoglou and Christian Egenhofer, October 2005

No. 55 *Towards a Global Climate Regime: Priority Areas for a Coherent EU Strategy*, Christian Egenhofer and Louise van Schaik, May 2005

No. 54 *EU Financial Regulation and Supervision beyond 2005*, Karel Lannoo and Jean-Pierre Casey, February 2005

No. 53 *Business Consequences of the EU Emissions Trading Scheme*, Christian Egenhofer, Noriko Fujiwara and Kyriakos Gialoglou, February 2005

* Available for purchase at http://shop.ceps.be